CYBERSECURITY

A DIGITAL DEFENSE GUIDE
FOR
BUSINESS LEADERS AND
BOARD DIRECTORS

ARVIND MEHTA

First Edition
Copyright © 2024
ISBN 13: 979-8-333-34015-3

The right of Arvind Mehta to be identified as author of this work has been asserted by him in accordance with the U.S. Copyright Act of 1976.

All rights reserved. No part of this publication may be reproduced, stored in retrieval system, or transmitted in any form or by any means, electronic, mechanical, photocopying, recording including but not limited to, in any network or other electronic storage or transmission, or broadcast for distance learning or otherwise, without the prior written permission of the author.

You may use the work for your own noncommercial and personal use; any other use of the work is strictly prohibited. Your right to use the work may be terminated if you fail to comply with these terms.

All trademarks used in the book are the properties of their respective owners. The use of any trademark in this text does not vest in the author any trademark ownership rights in such trademarks, nor does the use of such trademarks imply any affiliation with or endorsement of this book by such owners.

This book is written solely for informative purpose. Author of the book will not be responsible for any tangible or intangible damage caused by the information provided in this book.

ACKNOWLEDGEMENTS

The completion of this book, "CYBERSECURITY: A Digital Defense Guide For Business Leaders And Board Directors," marks a significant milestone in my professional journey. It is with immense gratitude and deep appreciation that I acknowledge the invaluable contributions of several individuals whose support, insights, and expertise have been instrumental in shaping the content and direction of this work.

First and foremost, I extend my heartfelt thanks to **Pankit Desai**, the CEO of Sequretek. Pankit's unwavering support and profound knowledge in the field of cybersecurity have been a cornerstone in the development of this book. His visionary leadership and dedication to advancing cybersecurity solutions have provided me with a wealth of information and a solid foundation upon which to build.

I am equally grateful to **Anand Naik**, CO-CEO of Sequretek, whose strategic insights and comprehensive understanding of cybersecurity have enriched this book immensely. Anand's commitment to innovation and his ability to foresee emerging cyber threats have significantly influenced the direction and scope of this guide.

My deepest appreciation goes to **Lalit Shinde**, the CRO of Sequretek, for his invaluable contributions. Lalit's expertise in risk management and his keen understanding of the cybersecurity landscape have been crucial in shaping the practical advice and strategies presented in this book. His guidance has ensured that the content is not only informative but also actionable for business leaders and board directors.

I am profoundly thankful to **Gopal Parvathaneni**, the CEO of EPSoft Inc., for his unwavering support and encouragement throughout this project. Gopal's deep knowledge of digital transformation and intelligent automation has provided a unique perspective on integrating cybersecurity with broader business strategies, adding significant value to this book.

I would also like to extend my sincere gratitude to **Mel Reyes**, former Global CIO & CISO of GetAround and former VP, IT Enterprise

Security & Authentication Program at Synchrony. Mel's extensive experience in enterprise security and his practical insights into crafting cybersecurity policies have been instrumental in ensuring that this guide addresses the most pressing cybersecurity challenges faced by businesses today. His willingness to share his expertise and experiences has greatly enhanced the quality and relevance of this book.

Finally, I am indebted to all my colleagues, friends, and family who have supported me in this endeavor. Their patience, encouragement, and belief in my vision have been a constant source of motivation.

This book is a collective effort, reflecting the shared knowledge and expertise of all these remarkable individuals. It is my sincere hope that "CYBERSECURITY: A Digital Defense Guide For Business Leaders And Board Directors" will serve as a valuable resource for those seeking to navigate the complex and ever-evolving landscape of cybersecurity.

Thank you all for your unwavering support and contributions.

PURPOSE OF THE BOOK

In today's digital age, the significance of robust cybersecurity measures cannot be overstated. Cyber threats are evolving at an unprecedented pace, targeting businesses of all sizes and across all industries. As a result, cybersecurity has become a critical concern not only for IT professionals but also for business leaders, non-tech executives, and board directors. These stakeholders are increasingly required to understand and manage the risks associated with digital threats to safeguard their organizations' assets, reputation, and regulatory compliance.

This book is designed to bridge the knowledge gap between technical cybersecurity experts and non-technical corporate leaders. This book aims to demystify the complex world of cybersecurity, providing essential insights and practical guidance tailored to those who may not have a deep technical background but hold significant responsibility for their organization's cybersecurity posture.

The primary objectives of this book are:

1. **Awareness and Understanding**: To raise awareness among business leaders about the critical importance of cybersecurity. By understanding the various types of cyber threats, the book helps leaders recognize potential risks and the consequences of security breaches.

2. **Practical Guidance**: To offer practical, actionable steps that can be implemented to enhance an organization's cybersecurity defenses. This includes strategies for developing and enforcing cybersecurity policies, managing cybersecurity teams, and integrating cybersecurity into the overall business strategy.

3. **Regulatory Compliance**: To educate readers about the regulatory landscape related to cybersecurity. With regulations such as Sarbanes-Oxley (SOX) and the SEC's new requirement for disclosing cybersecurity breaches within four

business days, it is crucial for business leaders to understand their legal obligations and how to ensure compliance.

4. **Risk Management**: To provide tools and frameworks for assessing and managing cybersecurity risks. This includes understanding the cost-benefit analysis of different security investments and making informed decisions to protect the organization effectively.

5. **Leadership and Governance**: To emphasize the role of leadership and governance in building a strong cybersecurity culture. This includes guidance on how board directors and senior executives can champion cybersecurity initiatives, allocate resources effectively, and foster a security-conscious environment.

By the end of this book, readers will be equipped with the knowledge and tools needed to navigate the complex cybersecurity landscape. They will understand how to protect their organizations against cyber threats, ensure regulatory compliance, and leverage intelligent automation to enhance their cybersecurity defenses. This book is a critical resource for business leaders committed to safeguarding their digital assets and maintaining the trust of their stakeholders in an increasingly connected world.

Table of Contents

PART I: CYBERSECURITY FUNDAMENTALS

1 Introduction — 15
Why I Decided to Write This Book
The Purpose This Book Solves
Why This Book Is a Must Read

2 Understanding Cybersecurity — 19
Definition and Importance
History and Evolution

3 Types of Cyber Threats — 21
Malware
Phishing
Sand Dune and Sand Worm
Whale-phishing Attacks
Spear-phishing Attacks
Password Attacks
SQL Injection Attacks
URL Interpretation
DNS Spoofing
Session Hijacking
Brute Force Attacks
Cross-site Scripting (XSS) and
Cross-site Request Forgery (CSRF) Attacks
Drive-by Attacks
Trojan Horses
Eavesdropping Attacks
Birthday Attacks
Ransomware
Denial-of-Service (DoS) Attacks
Distributed Denial-of-Service (DDoS) Attacks
Man-in-the-Middle (MITM) Attacks
Insider Threats
Advanced Persistent Threats (APTs)

4 Cybersecurity Concepts — 29
Confidentiality, Integrity, Availability (CIA Triad)

Authentication and Authorization
Encryption
Firewalls and Antivirus Software

5 Cybersecurity Frameworks and Standards — 31
NIST Cybersecurity Framework
ISO/IEC 27001
CIS Controls
COBIT
MITRE ATT&CK Framework
SOC2 Controls

6 Types of Cybersecurity — 35

6.1 Network Security
Network Segmentation
Virtual Private Networks (VPNs)
Intrusion Detection and Prevention Systems (IDPS)

6.2 Endpoint Security
Securing Devices
Mobile Device Management (MDM)
Patch Management

6.3 Application Security
Secure Software Development Life Cycle (SDLC)
Common Vulnerabilities and Exposures (CVE)
Web Application Firewalls (WAF)

6.4 Cloud Security
Shared Responsibility Model
Data Protection in the Cloud
Identity and Access Management (IAM)

7 Advanced Cybersecurity Concepts — 41
Managed Detection and Response (MDR)
Endpoint Detection and Response (EDR)
Incident Detection and Response (IDR)
Extended Detection and Response (XDR)
Security Operations Center (SOC)
Zero Trust Model

Privileged Access Management (PAM)
Zero-Day Vulnerabilities
Simplified Endpoint Security
Identity and Access Governance (IAG)
Enterprise Cyber Defense
Checkpoints
Disaster Recovery and Incident Response
Security Orchestration, Automation, and Response (SOAR)
Identity Threat Detection and Response (ITDR)
Network Threat Detection and Response (NTDR)
User and Entity Behavior Analytics (UEBA)
Threat Hunter
Managed Threat Intelligence and Response (MTIR)
The Open Web Application Security Project (OWASP)
Network Analyzers
Other Advanced Cybersecurity Technologies

8 Security Information and Event Management   55
Introduction to SIEM
Functions of SIEM
SIEM Integration with XDR

9 Incident Response and Management   57
Incident Response Plan
Forensics and Investigation
Recovery and Lessons Learned

**10 Enterprise-wide Threat Detection   61
and Response Landscape**

11 Cybersecurity Best Practices   67
User Training and Awareness
Implement Strong Password Policies
Enable MFA
Regular Update and Patch Systems
Regular Audits and Assessments
Use Firewall and Antivirus
Secure Remote Work
Backup Data Regularly
Implement Least Privileged Access
Develop and Enforce Robust IRP

Risk Response, Mitigation, and Control
Ten Rules of Operational Security (OpSec)

12 Tracking and Privacy Concerns 73
How We Are Tracked Online
SSD Forensics
Door Locks and Access Badge Cloning

13 Interoperability Issues 75
Challenges with Multiple Devices
Solutions for Interoperability

PART II: DIGITAL DEFENSE GUIDE FOR BUSINESS LEADERS AND BOARD DIRECTORS

14 Introduction to Cybersecurity for Board Directors   79
Importance of Cybersecurity in Corporate Governance
The Evolving Threat Landscape
Role of Board Directors

15 Board Directors' Responsibilities in Cybersecurity   83
Fiduciary Duties and Cybersecurity
Legal and Regulatory Obligations
Ethical Considerations

16 Risk Assessment and Management   91
Impact of Cyber Incidents on Business Continuity and Reputation
Strategies for Effective Risk Management

17 Building a Cybersecurity Culture   95
Promoting Cyber Awareness and Training
Encouraging a Security-First Mindset
Collaboration Between IT and Other Departments

18 Developing a Cybersecurity Strategy   99
Setting Cybersecurity Objectives and Goals
Aligning Cybersecurity with Business Strategy
Resource Allocation for Cybersecurity Initiatives
Incident Response and Disaster Recovery Planning

19 Cybersecurity Policy Making   103
Building a Robust Cybersecurity Strategy
Developing Comprehensive Cybersecurity Policies
Policy Implementation and Enforcement
Regular Review and Updates

20 Governance Structures for Cybersecurity   109
Roles and Responsibilities of the Board and Executive Management
Establishing Cybersecurity Committees
Reporting and Accountability Mechanisms

21 Role of Board Directors in Cyber-Risk Management — 117
Identifying and Mitigating Cyber Risks
Risk Management Frameworks and Tools
Integrating Cyber Risk into Enterprise Risk Management
Incident Response and Crisis Management

22 Incident Response and Disaster Recovery — 123
Developing and Implementing Incident Response Plans
Crisis Management, Business Continuity and Disaster Recovery
Disaster Recovery Planning and Execution

23 Cybersecurity Metrics and Reporting — 133
Key Performance Indicators (KPIs) for Cybersecurity
Reporting Cybersecurity Metrics to the Board
Using Metrics for Decision-Making and Oversight

24 Engaging with External Experts — 139
Collaborating with Cybersecurity Consultants and Advisors
Leveraging Industry Partnerships and Networks
Understanding the Role of External Audits and Assessments

25 Examples of Some Practical Scenarios — 145
Scenario 1: A Cybersecurity Disaster Averted
Scenario 2: Incident Management and Damage Mitigation
Scenario 3: Enhancing Cyber Resilience Through Board Initiatives
Scenario 4: Cybersecurity Breach and Legal Ramifications

26 Future Trends in Cybersecurity — 151
Emerging Technologies and Their Impact on Cybersecurity
Preparing for Future Cyber Threats
AI-Powered Cybersecurity Platforms
The Role of Board Directors in Shaping the Future of Cybersecurity

27 Epilogue — 159

PART I

CYBERSECURITY FUNDAMENTALS

1. Introduction

In the summer of 2023, I received an urgent call from a friend, the CEO of an angel investor-backed technology firm that had been bootstrapped since its inception. This company was on the brink of launching its first round of capital raising—a pivotal moment for its growth and future prospects. However, their plans were abruptly derailed by a significant cyber-attack. The breach compromised sensitive customer data and disrupted their operations, forcing them to delay their fundraising process. This delay cost the company a crucial opportunity, as they missed the "right timing" to attract potential investors who were initially very interested.

Why I Decided to Write This Book

Reflecting on that incident, I realized that many executives and board members, despite their expertise in other areas, often feel overwhelmed by the complexities of cybersecurity. The language of cyber threats, risks, and defenses can seem like an impenetrable jargon-laden world reserved for IT specialists. Yet, the consequences of cyber incidents have far-reaching implications that transcend the technical realm, affecting corporate reputation, financial stability, and regulatory compliance.

Driven by this realization, I embarked on a mission to bridge the knowledge gap between technical cybersecurity measures and strategic business decision-making. This book is the culmination of that mission. It is crafted to demystify cybersecurity, providing you with the essential knowledge and tools to navigate the digital threats facing your organization.

The Purpose This Book Solves

In an era where digital threats are constantly evolving, understanding cybersecurity is no longer optional for business leaders—it is essential. This book serves multiple purposes:

1. **Educating Non-Tech Leaders:** It translates complex cybersecurity concepts into accessible, actionable insights tailored for non-technical executives and board members.

2. **Strategic Decision-Making:** It equips you with the knowledge to make informed strategic decisions, ensuring that cybersecurity is integrated into your overall business strategy.

3. **Compliance and Risk Management:** It provides a comprehensive overview of relevant cybersecurity laws, regulations, and standards, helping you navigate the compliance landscape and mitigate risks effectively.

4. **Building Resilience:** It offers practical guidance on developing robust cybersecurity policies, incident response plans, and risk management frameworks to enhance your organization's resilience against cyber threats.

Why This Book is a Must-Read

During my long career in IT, I have seen firsthand the devastating impact that cyber incidents can have on businesses. My diverse professional background, spanning various industries, has provided me with a unique perspective on the multifaceted nature of cybersecurity challenges.

This book is a must-read for several reasons:

1. **Holistic Perspective:** It combines technical knowledge with strategic insights, offering a holistic approach to cybersecurity that is tailored for business leaders, non-tech executives, and board directors.

2. **Real-World Examples:** It draws on real-world case studies and examples to illustrate key points, making the content relatable and practical.

3. **Expert Insights:** It leverages my extensive experience and expertise, as well as insights from leading cybersecurity professionals, to provide you with cutting-edge knowledge and best practices.

4. **Actionable Guidance:** It offers clear, actionable guidance on how to implement effective cybersecurity measures, from governance and risk management to incident response and compliance.

Cybersecurity is an ever-present and evolving challenge that requires the attention and involvement of every leader within an organization. This book is designed to empower you with the knowledge and tools needed to protect your organization from digital threats and ensure its long-term success. Together, let us navigate the complexities of cybersecurity and build a safer, more resilient digital future for our businesses.

2. Understanding Cybersecurity

In today's digital age, cybersecurity has become a critical aspect of our daily lives. As we increasingly rely on technology for communication, work, and entertainment, the need to protect our data and systems from malicious attacks has never been greater. This comprehensive tutorial aims to provide a detailed understanding of cybersecurity, its importance, and how individuals and organizations can safeguard their digital assets.

Definition and Importance

Cybersecurity refers to the practice of protecting systems, networks, and data from digital attacks. These cyberattacks are often aimed at accessing, changing, or destroying sensitive information, extorting money from users, or interrupting normal business processes. The importance of cybersecurity cannot be overstated as it is essential for protecting personal information, maintaining privacy, and ensuring the integrity and availability of data.

History and Evolution

The concept of cybersecurity dates back to the early days of computing in the 1970s when the first computer viruses appeared. Over the decades, cybersecurity has evolved in response to the growing sophistication of cyber threats. Today, it encompasses a wide range of practices, technologies, and regulations designed to combat an ever-evolving landscape of digital threats.

20

3. Types of Cyber Threats

Cyber threats vary widely, from straightforward scams like an email promising wealth in exchange for sensitive banking information, to sophisticated stealth attacks where malicious code evades detection and resides within networks for extended periods, eventually leading to costly data breaches. The more awareness security teams and employees have of these diverse cybersecurity threats, the better equipped they are to prevent, prepare for, and respond to cyberattacks. These threats evolve rapidly, with tactics and attack methods continuously advancing. Cybercriminals exploit various avenues, known as **attack vectors**, to gain unauthorized access to computers or network servers and cause harm. Below are the most common types of cyber threats:

Malware Attacks short for malicious software, are designed to damage or disable computers and systems. It includes viruses, worms, Trojan horses, and spyware. These malicious programs can steal, encrypt, or delete sensitive data, alter or hijack core computing functions, and monitor users' computer activity without their permission.

Phishing Attacks is a type of social engineering attack often used to steal user data, including login credentials and credit card numbers. It occurs when an attacker masquerades as a trusted entity and tricks a victim into opening an email, instant message, or text message.

Sand Dune and Sand Worm

These terms refer to specific cyber threats:

- **Sand Dune:** A sophisticated malware family targeting government and defense entities. It often involves advanced techniques to evade detection.

- **Sand Worm**: A notable cyber-espionage group associated with Russian state-sponsored activities. They are known for their targeted attacks on critical infrastructure.

Whale-phishing Attacks target high-profile individuals or executives with personalized messages, aiming to deceive them into divulging sensitive information or performing actions that compromise security, leveraging their authority or access within an organization.

Spear-phishing Attacks are highly targeted email scams that tailor messages to specific individuals or groups, often using personal information to increase credibility. They aim to trick recipients into revealing confidential data or clicking on malicious links, exploiting trust to breach organizational defenses.

Password Attacks involve various methods to crack passwords, including **brute force attacks** (trying numerous combinations), **dictionary attacks** (using common words or phrases), or phishing schemes designed to trick users into revealing passwords, compromising account security.

SQL Injection Attacks exploit vulnerabilities in web applications by inserting malicious SQL code into input fields. This code can manipulate databases, retrieve sensitive information, or even delete data, depending on the attacker's objectives and the system's security measures.

URL Interpretation vulnerabilities occur when web browsers or applications incorrectly parse or interpret URLs, leading to unintended consequences such as redirecting users to malicious websites or executing unintended actions based on manipulated URLs.

DNS Spoofing involves falsifying DNS records to redirect traffic from legitimate servers to malicious ones controlled by attackers. This can lead users to unintentionally interact with fraudulent websites or services, compromising their security.

Session Hijacking exploits weaknesses in session management to steal active session tokens or cookies, allowing attackers to impersonate legitimate users and gain unauthorized access to sensitive accounts or systems.

Brute Force Attacks systematically try numerous combinations of passwords or encryption keys until the correct one is found, exploiting weaknesses in authentication systems that lack sufficient safeguards against repeated login attempts.

Cross-site Scripting (XSS) and Cross-site Request Forgery (CSRF) Attacks manipulate vulnerable web applications to execute malicious scripts in users' browsers or forge unauthorized requests, respectively. These attacks can steal user credentials, manipulate web content, or perform actions on behalf of authenticated users without their consent.

Drive-by Attacks exploit vulnerabilities in web browsers or plugins to automatically download malware onto users' devices when visiting compromised websites, often without their knowledge or interaction, compromising system security.

Trojan Horses are malicious programs disguised as legitimate software. Once installed, they enable unauthorized access or perform harmful actions, such as stealing data, disrupting operations, or giving attackers remote control over infected systems.

Eavesdropping Attacks involve intercepting and monitoring data transmissions, such as network traffic or communication channels, to capture sensitive information without the knowledge or consent of the communicating parties, compromising confidentiality.

Birthday Attacks exploit cryptographic hash functions' vulnerabilities by leveraging the birthday paradox to find collisions (two different inputs producing the same hash). This can undermine integrity checks, digital signatures, or other security mechanisms relying on hash functions.

Ransomware is a type of malware that threatens to publish the victim's data or block access to it unless a ransom is paid. This type of attack can be devastating for individuals and organizations, leading to significant financial loss and operational disruption.

Denial-of-Service (DoS) Attacks aim to shut down a machine or network, making it inaccessible to its intended users. DoS attacks accomplish this by flooding the target with traffic or sending it information that triggers a crash.

Distributed Denial-of-Service (DDoS) Attacks In a Distributed Denial-of-Service (DDoS) attack, multiple systems are used to launch a coordinated attack against a single target. This can overwhelm the target with traffic from multiple sources, making it even more difficult to mitigate than a traditional DoS attack.

Man-in-the-Middle (MITM) Attacks occur when an attacker secretly intercepts and relays messages between two parties who believe they are communicating directly with each other. This type of attack can be used to steal personal information, such as login credentials and credit card numbers.

Insider Threats involve someone within an organization who has access to the organization's assets and exploits this access to harm the organization. This can be a current or former employee, contractor, or business partner.

Advanced Persistent Threats (APTs) are a type of cyberattack where unauthorized users gain access to a network and remain undetected for an extended period. These threats are sophisticated, resource-intensive, and typically aim to steal data or surveil networks rather than causing immediate damage.

Characteristics

1. **Advanced**: Uses continuous, sophisticated, and targeted attack techniques. Attackers often employ various methods such as zero-day exploits, spear-phishing, and custom malware

2. **Persistent**: Focuses on maintaining long-term access to the target's network to continuously extract data. The attackers may re-enter the network multiple times to achieve their objective.

3. **Threat**: Involves human operators, as opposed to automated programs, making decisions and adapting tactics to achieve specific goals.

Phases of an APT Attack

1. **Initial Entry**: Attackers gain access to the target network through methods such as phishing, exploiting vulnerabilities, or using social engineering tactics.

2. **Establish Foothold**: Install backdoors and malware to maintain access. They may also use legitimate credentials obtained during the initial breach.

3. **Escalate Privileges**: Gain higher-level access to broaden their reach within the network. This involves finding and exploiting additional vulnerabilities to gain administrator rights.

4. **Internal Reconnaissance**: Explore the network, identifying critical systems and sensitive data. Attackers map out the network architecture and identify valuable assets.

5. **Lateral Movement**: Move through the network to access additional systems and data. This often involves using stolen credentials and exploiting trust relationships between systems.

6. **Data Exfiltration**: Steal sensitive data over an extended period, often using encrypted channels to avoid detection. The data is then transferred to external servers controlled by the attackers.

7. **Cover Tracks**: Maintain stealth by deleting logs, hiding files, and using other techniques to avoid detection and removal.

Common Techniques and Tools

- **Spear Phishing**: Crafting targeted emails to trick users into divulging credentials or downloading malware.

- **Zero-Day Exploits**: Exploiting vulnerabilities that are unknown to the vendor or have no available patch.

- **Custom Malware**: Developing unique malware tailored to the specific target environment.

- **Command and Control (C2) Servers**: Using external servers to control infected machines and exfiltrate data.

- **Credential Dumping**: Extracting password hashes and other authentication tokens from compromised systems.

- **Lateral Movement Tools**: Utilizing tools like Mimikatz for credential harvesting and PsExec for executing commands on remote systems.

Real-World Examples

- **Stuxnet**: A sophisticated worm targeting Iran's nuclear facilities, designed to sabotage industrial control systems.

- **APT1 (Comment Crew)**: A Chinese cyber espionage group linked to numerous attacks on Western organizations, primarily targeting intellectual property.

- **Equation Group**: Associated with the NSA, known for deploying highly sophisticated malware like the EquationDrug and DoubleFantasy.

Defense and Mitigation Strategies

1. **Network Segmentation**: Limiting the ability of attackers to move laterally within a network.

2. **Regular Software Updates**: Keeping systems patched to close vulnerabilities that could be exploited.

3. **User Education**: Training employees to recognize phishing attempts and other social engineering tactics.

4. **Advanced Threat Detection**: Implementing solutions like Intrusion Detection Systems (IDS), Intrusion Prevention Systems (IPS), and Security Information and Event Management (SIEM) to monitor and respond to suspicious activities.

5. **Multi-Factor Authentication (MFA)**: Adding an additional layer of security beyond just usernames and passwords.

6. **Incident Response Plans**: Preparing for potential breaches with a clear strategy for containment and remediation.

APTs represent a significant threat due to their sophistication and potential for causing long-term damage. Effective defense requires a combination of advanced detection technologies, proactive security measures, and user education to mitigate the risks associated with these persistent and adaptive threats.

4. Cybersecurity Concepts

Confidentiality, Integrity, Availability (CIA Triad)

The CIA triad is a fundamental concept in cybersecurity that guides policies for information security within an organization. It consists of:

- **Confidentiality:** Ensuring that information is accessible only to those authorized to have access.

- **Integrity:** Maintaining the accuracy and completeness of data over its lifecycle.

- **Availability:** Ensuring that information and resources are available to authorized users when needed.

Authentication and Authorization

Authentication is the process of verifying the identity of a user, device, or entity attempting to access a system, ensuring they are who they claim to be while Authorization is the process of giving someone permission to do or have something. It determines the level of access granted to authenticated users. These processes are critical for ensuring that only authorized individuals can access sensitive information.

Encryption

Encryption is the process of converting information or data into a code to prevent unauthorized access. It is one of the most effective ways to achieve data security, ensuring that even if data is intercepted, it cannot be read without the decryption key.

Firewalls and Antivirus Software

Firewalls are network security devices that monitor and filter incoming and outgoing network traffic based on an organization's previously established security policies. Antivirus software is designed to detect and destroy computer viruses and other malicious software.

The importance of cybersecurity, including these core concepts, cannot be overstated as cyber threats continue to evolve in complexity and scale, posing significant risks to individuals, businesses, and governments. Ensuring robust cybersecurity measures is fundamental not only to prevent financial losses and operational disruptions but also to maintain trust and compliance with regulatory requirements. As the digital landscape expands, the role of cybersecurity becomes increasingly vital in defending against a myriad of threats, thus securing the foundation of our digital society.

5. Cybersecurity Frameworks and Standards

NIST Cybersecurity Framework

The National Institute of Standards and Technology (NIST) Cybersecurity Framework provides a policy framework of computer security guidance for how private sector organizations in the US can assess and improve their ability to prevent, detect, and respond to cyberattacks. The framework comprises five core functions: Identify, Protect, Detect, Respond, and Recover.

ISO/IEC 27001

International Organization for Standardization (ISO) and the International Electrotechnical Commission (IEC) ISO/IEC 27001 is an international standard for managing information security. It provides a framework for an Information Security Management System (ISMS) to help organizations make their information assets more secure.

CIS Controls

The Center for Internet Security (CIS) Controls are a set of best practices for securing IT systems and data against the most pervasive attacks. They are developed by a global community of cybersecurity experts. The CIS Controls are a set of 20 actionable guidelines designed to help organizations improve their cybersecurity posture. These controls prioritize and focus on specific actions within a smaller number of areas with high pay-off results.

COBIT (Control Objectives for Information and Related Technologies)

ISACA's (Information Systems Audit and Control Association) COBIT framework is for developing, implementing, monitoring, and improving IT governance and management practices. It helps organizations achieve their strategic goals and deliver value through effective governance and management of IT.

MITRE ATT&CK (Adversarial Tactics, Techniques, and Common Knowledge) Framework

The MITRE ATT&CK is framework created by MITRE Corporation. It is a critical component of modern cybersecurity strategies. It is a globally accessible knowledge base of adversary tactics and techniques based on real-world observations. It is used by cybersecurity professionals to understand, detect, and respond to cyber threats.

Key Features of the MITRE ATT&CK Framework:

1. **Adversary Behaviors:** The framework categorizes the behaviors and techniques that adversaries use throughout different stages of an attack lifecycle, providing detailed insights into how threats manifest in real-world environments.

2. **Tactics and Techniques:** ATT&CK is structured around tactics (the why of an attack) and techniques (the how). This helps organizations understand the specific methods adversaries might use to achieve their objectives, such as gaining initial access, executing malicious code, or exfiltrating data.

3. **Sub-Techniques:** These provide further granularity, detailing the specific implementations of broader techniques. This allows for more precise detection and mitigation strategies.

4. **Mitigations and Detection:** The framework offers guidance on how to mitigate and detect various techniques, providing

practical steps organizations can take to protect their environments.

5. **ATT&CK Navigator:** A tool that allows cybersecurity professionals to visualize and manipulate ATT&CK data to better understand and apply it within their own environments.

Why is the MITRE ATT&CK Framework Important?

1. **Threat Intelligence:** It provides a comprehensive repository of threat intelligence, helping organizations understand the tactics and techniques used by adversaries in the wild.

2. **Defensive Planning:** By understanding potential attack vectors, organizations can better plan and prioritize their defensive measures, focusing on the most relevant threats.

3. **Incident Response:** ATT&CK serves as a valuable reference during incident response, enabling responders to quickly identify and correlate adversary behaviors to known tactics and techniques, thereby speeding up the investigation process.

4. **Red Teaming:** Security teams can use the framework to simulate real-world attack scenarios, testing their defenses and identifying gaps in their security posture.

5. **Threat Hunting:** The detailed breakdown of adversary behaviors allows threat hunters to develop more effective and targeted hunting queries, improving the likelihood of detecting advanced threats.

6. **Standardization:** ATT&CK provides a common language for describing adversary behavior, facilitating better communication and collaboration within and across organizations.

Integration Example:

- **Detection and Monitoring:** A financial institution might use the MITRE ATT&CK Framework to enhance their Security Information and Event Management (SIEM) system by mapping detected behaviors to specific ATT&CK techniques. This improves their ability to detect and respond to sophisticated cyber-attacks.

- **Threat Hunting:** A healthcare organization might develop specific threat hunting queries based on ATT&CK techniques known to target healthcare systems, enabling proactive detection of potential intrusions.

The MITRE ATT&CK Framework is an essential tool for modern cybersecurity, providing detailed insights into adversary behaviors and practical guidance for defending against them. It complements other cybersecurity frameworks by offering a granular, behavior-based approach to understanding and mitigating cyber threats.

SOC2 Controls

SOC 2 (Service Organization Control 2) controls are a set of criteria established by the American Institute of Certified Public Accountants (AICPA) for managing customer data based on five "trust service principles"—security, availability, processing integrity, confidentiality, and privacy. It's an auditing procedure designed to ensure that third party service providers manage and protect client information appropriately. The SOC 2 framework is specifically tailored for technology and cloud computing organizations, helping them demonstrate their commitment to secure data handling and processing. Each principle encompasses various criteria and controls, such as access controls, system operations, monitoring, and risk mitigation strategies, to ensure robust information security and compliance. Security controls focus on preventing unauthorized access to systems and data, employing measures like multi-factor authentication, encryption, and regular vulnerability assessments. Availability controls ensure systems are reliable and can recover from disruptions, incorporating redundancy and disaster recovery plans.

6. Types of Cybersecurity

In today's interconnected digital landscape, cybersecurity stands as a cornerstone of safeguarding systems, networks, and data against a spectrum of malicious threats. From robust network security protocols that shield against unauthorized access and data breaches to vigilant application security measures that defend against vulnerabilities in software and web applications, and endpoint security solutions that protect individual devices from malware and unauthorized access, each facet of cybersecurity plays a pivotal role in preserving the integrity and confidentiality of digital assets. As technology evolves, so too do the methods employed by cyber adversaries, making a comprehensive understanding of these cybersecurity domains essential for effectively mitigating risks and ensuring resilience in the face of evolving threats.

6.1 Network Security

Network Segmentation

Network segmentation involves dividing a computer network into smaller parts, or segments, to improve performance and security. It helps in limiting access to sensitive data and reduces the risk of cyberattacks spreading across the entire network.

Virtual Private Networks (VPNs)

VPNs create a secure, encrypted connection over a less secure network, such as the internet. They are used to protect the privacy of data transmissions, ensuring that sensitive information is not intercepted by unauthorized parties.

Intrusion Detection and Prevention Systems (IDPS)

IDPS are systems used to monitor network traffic for suspicious activity and potential threats. Intrusion detection systems (IDS) alert administrators of potential attacks, while intrusion prevention systems (IPS) actively block threats from reaching the network.

6.2 Endpoint Security

Securing Devices

Endpoint security involves securing end-user devices such as computers, laptops, and mobile devices. This includes implementing security measures like antivirus software, firewalls, and device encryption.

Mobile Device Management (MDM)

MDM is a type of security software used to monitor, manage, and secure employees' mobile devices across an organization. It ensures that mobile devices comply with the organization's security policies and protects against data breaches.

Patch Management

Patch management involves the process of distributing and applying updates to software. These patches often fix security vulnerabilities and other bugs, helping to protect systems from attacks.

6.3 Application Security

Secure Software Development Life Cycle (SDLC)

The Secure SDLC is a process that integrates security into every phase of the software development life cycle. This includes planning, design, implementation, testing, deployment, and maintenance.

Common Vulnerabilities and Exposures (CVE)

CVE is a list of publicly disclosed computer security flaws. When someone refers to a CVE identifier, they mean a specific vulnerability that has been assigned a CVE ID.

Web Application Firewalls (WAF)

WAFs are security systems designed to protect web applications by filtering and monitoring HTTP traffic between a web application and the internet. They help protect against attacks such as cross-site scripting (XSS) and SQL injection.

6.4 Cloud Security

Shared Responsibility Model

In cloud security, the shared responsibility model defines the security responsibilities of the cloud service provider and the customer. While providers manage the security of the cloud, customers are responsible for securing their data within the cloud. It clarifies who is responsible for securing what components of the cloud infrastructure, including data, applications, operating systems, networks, and physical security.

Key Components of the Model

1. **Cloud Provider Responsibilities:**

   - **Physical Infrastructure Security:** CSPs are responsible for securing their physical data centers, including network infrastructure, servers, and storage.

   - **Platform Security:** They manage the security of the cloud platform itself, including the hardware and software that run the services.

2. **Customer Responsibilities:**

   - **Data:** Customers are accountable for the security of their data—how it is accessed, stored, and managed within the cloud environment.

   - **Applications:** Securing applications and ensuring they are configured correctly falls under the customer's responsibility.

   - **Identity and Access Management (IAM):** Customers must manage access to their cloud resources, implementing appropriate authentication and authorization protocols.

   - **Network Traffic:** Configuring firewalls, monitoring traffic, and securing network connections are tasks handled by the customer.

Data Protection in the Cloud: Ensuring Security and Compliance

As businesses increasingly migrate their operations to the cloud, ensuring robust data protection measures becomes paramount. Cloud computing offers numerous benefits, including scalability, flexibility, and cost-efficiency, but it also introduces unique challenges and risks related to data security. Understanding how to effectively protect data in the cloud is essential for maintaining trust with customers, complying with regulations, and safeguarding against cyber threats.

Challenges of Data Protection in the Cloud

1. **Data Breaches:** Cloud environments can be targets for cyberattacks aiming to exploit vulnerabilities in infrastructure, applications, or misconfigured settings.

2. **Data Loss:** Accidental deletion, service outages, or operational errors can lead to data loss if not properly mitigated with backup and recovery strategies.

3. **Compliance Requirements:** Different industries and regions have stringent regulations governing data privacy and

protection, such as GDPR in Europe or HIPAA in the healthcare sector in the United States.

Best Practices for Data Protection in the Cloud

1. **Encryption:** Encrypting data both at rest and in transit ensures that even if unauthorized parties gain access, they cannot decipher the information without the encryption keys.

2. **Access Control:** Implementing robust identity and access management (IAM) policies ensures that only authorized users and devices can access sensitive data. This includes using multi-factor authentication (MFA) and least privilege principles.

3. **Data Backup and Recovery:** Regularly backing up data to separate, secure locations ensures that data can be restored in the event of data corruption, deletion, or ransomware attacks.

4. **Monitoring and Logging:** Implementing continuous monitoring and logging of activities within the cloud environment helps detect suspicious behavior or unauthorized access attempts promptly.

5. **Compliance Management:** Stay informed about relevant data protection regulations and ensure that cloud service providers (CSPs) comply with these standards. This includes reviewing CSP contracts and conducting audits as necessary.

Cloud Service Provider (CSP) Responsibilities

1. **Security "of" the Cloud Infrastructure:** CSPs are responsible for securing the underlying cloud infrastructure, including physical servers, networking, and hypervisors.

2. **Security "in" the Cloud:** Customers are responsible for securing their data, applications, identities, and access management within the cloud environment.

Protecting data in the cloud requires a proactive and multi-layered approach that combines technology, policies, and collaboration between cloud providers and customers. By understanding the unique challenges and implementing best practices outlined above, businesses can mitigate risks, ensure compliance, and maintain the integrity and confidentiality of their data in the cloud. As technology evolves, staying informed about emerging threats and adopting new security measures will be crucial in safeguarding sensitive information in an increasingly digital world.

Identity and Access Management (IAM)

IAM involves managing digital identities and controlling access to resources. It ensures that the right individuals have the appropriate access to technology resources. Key components include:

- **Authentication:** Verifying the identity of users (e.g., passwords, biometrics).

- **Authorization:** Granting permissions based on user roles.

- **Single Sign-On (SSO):** Allows users to log in once and access multiple systems without re-authenticating.

7. Advanced Cybersecurity Concepts

Managed Detection and Response (MDR)

MDR is a service that provides organizations with threat detection and response capabilities. It combines technology and human expertise to identify and mitigate threats using:

- **24/7 monitoring:** Continuous surveillance of systems.
- **Threat intelligence:** Using data to predict and prevent attacks.
- **Incident response:** Actions taken to manage and mitigate security breaches.

Endpoint Detection and Response (EDR)

EDR focuses on detecting and investigating suspicious activities on endpoints (e.g., computers, mobile devices) using:

- **Real-time monitoring:** Constant surveillance of endpoints.
- **Behavioral analysis:** Identifying unusual patterns that may indicate threats.
- **Automated response:** Immediate actions to contain threats.

Incident Detection and Response (IDR)

IDR encompasses the processes and tools used to detect, investigate, and respond to security incidents. It involves:

- **Detection:** Identifying potential security events.
- **Investigation:** Analyzing the nature and impact of the event.
- **Response:** Taking corrective actions to mitigate the impact.

Extended Detection and Response (XDR)

XDR integrates multiple security products into a cohesive system for broader visibility and automated response using:

- **Cross-layer detection:** Combines data from various sources (network, endpoint, server).
- **Correlation of alerts:** Identifies complex threats across the entire IT environment.
- **Unified response:** Orchestrates automated actions to neutralize threats.

Security Operations Center (SOC)

A SOC is a centralized unit that deals with security issues on an organizational and technical level. It involves:

- **Monitoring and analysis:** Continuous surveillance of network traffic and endpoints.
- **Incident handling:** Coordinating responses to security breaches.
- **Threat intelligence:** Staying updated on current threats and vulnerabilities.

Zero Trust Model

The Zero Trust Model operates on the principle of "never trust, always verify." It assumes that threats can come from both outside and inside the network. It involves:

- **Least privilege access:** Users are given the minimum levels of access necessary.
- **Micro-segmentation:** Dividing the network into smaller zones to contain breaches.
- **Continuous monitoring:** Constantly verifying user and device credentials.

Privileged Access Management (PAM)

PAM involves controlling and monitoring access to critical systems by privileged users and involves:

- **Credential management:** Securely storing and managing administrative passwords.
- **Session monitoring:** Tracking and recording activities during privileged sessions.
- **Least privilege:** Ensuring users have the minimum necessary access.

Zero-Day Vulnerabilities

Zero-Day Vulnerabilities are security flaws unknown to the software vendor and without a patch:

- **Exploitation:** Cybercriminals exploit these vulnerabilities before they are patched.
- **Detection:** Requires advanced monitoring and anomaly detection techniques.
- **Mitigation:** Implementing layers of defense and prompt patching when updates are available.

Simplified Endpoint Security

Simplified Endpoint Security aims to make protecting devices (endpoints) easier and more effective through:

- **Unified solutions**: Integrates antivirus, anti-malware, and firewall into a single package.
- **Automation:** Uses AI and machine learning to detect and respond to threats automatically.
- **User-friendly interfaces**: Designed for ease of use, reducing the need for specialized knowledge.

Identity and Access Governance (IAG)

IAG ensures that identity management and access controls are aligned with organizational policies and regulatory requirements through:

- **Policy enforcement**: Ensures access policies are followed consistently.
- **Role management**: Defines and manages user roles and associated permissions.
- **Access reviews**: Regularly audits access rights to maintain compliance.

Enterprise Cyber Defense

Enterprise Cyber Defense involves comprehensive strategies and solutions to protect an organization's information systems using:

- **Threat intelligence**: Using data to anticipate and mitigate threats.
- **Advanced security tools**: Employing firewalls, intrusion detection/prevention systems, and endpoint security.
- **Incident response**: Preparing and executing plans to handle security incidents effectively.

Checkpoints

Checkpoints in cybersecurity refer to security points within a network where traffic is monitored and controlled:

- **Firewall checkpoints**: Inspect and filter traffic entering or leaving a network.
- **Security gateways**: Combine multiple security functions like VPN, firewall, and antivirus at key network junctures.

Disaster Recovery (DR) and Incident Response (IR)

Disaster Recovery and Incident Response are critical components of a cybersecurity strategy:

- **Disaster Recovery**: Plans and procedures to restore IT systems and data after a major incident.
- **Incident Response**: Steps taken to detect, respond to, and recover from security incidents, including:

- **Preparation**: Developing and testing response plans.
- **Detection and analysis**: Identifying and understanding the incident.
- **Containment, eradication, and recovery**: Limiting damage, eliminating threats, and restoring systems.

Security Orchestration, Automation, and Response (SOAR)

Security Orchestration, Automation, and Response (SOAR) is a collection of software solutions and tools that enable organizations to streamline their security operations in three key areas: threat and vulnerability management, incident response, and security operations automation. SOAR platforms integrate and coordinate disparate security technologies and processes, enhancing the efficiency and effectiveness of security operations.

SOAR is one of the most advanced technologies in cybersecurity. The concept of "most advanced" in cybersecurity can be subjective and context-dependent, as different technologies excel in different areas of cybersecurity.

Identity Threat Detection and Response (ITDR)

Identity Threat Detection and Response (ITDR) is a cybersecurity framework focusing on detecting and mitigating threats that target user identities and access credentials. ITDR solutions aim to:

- Monitor and analyze user behavior to detect anomalies
- Identify compromised accounts and credentials
- Implement policies and measures to prevent unauthorized access

Key Functions:

- Behavioral analytics
- Anomaly detection
- Multi-factor authentication enforcement
- Real-time threat response

Network Threat Detection and Response (NTDR)

Network Threat Detection and Response (NTDR) is designed to identify, analyze, and respond to threats within network traffic. NTDR solutions focus on:

- Monitoring network traffic for suspicious activities
- Detecting intrusions and advanced persistent threats (APTs)
- Providing real-time alerts and automated responses to threats

Key Functions:

- Deep packet inspection
- Traffic analysis
- Anomaly detection
- Automated response mechanisms

User and Entity Behavior Analytics (UEBA)

User and Entity Behavior Analytics (UEBA) involves the use of machine learning and analytics to monitor user and entity behavior within an organization. UEBA solutions:

- Establish baseline behavior patterns for users and entities (devices, applications, etc.)
- Detect deviations from normal behavior that may indicate a threat
- Provide context to security alerts to improve response accuracy

Key Functions:

- Behavioral baselines
- Anomaly detection
- Risk scoring
- Integration with SIEM and other security tools

Threat Hunter

Threat Hunter refers to the practice of proactively searching for cyber threats that may be lurking within a network. Threat hunters:

- Use a combination of automated tools and human analysis.
- Look for indicators of compromise (IOCs) and tactics, techniques, and procedures (TTPs) used by attackers.
- Focus on identifying and mitigating threats before they can cause damage.

Key Functions:

- Proactive threat identification.
- Manual and automated analysis.
- Collaboration with other security teams.
- Continuous improvement of detection techniques.

Managed Threat Intelligence and Response (MTIR)

Managed Threat Intelligence and Response (MTIR) services provide organizations with external threat intelligence and managed response capabilities. MTIR providers:

- Gather and analyze threat intelligence from various sources.
- Provide actionable insights and recommendations.
- Offer managed detection and response (MDR) services to handle incidents.

Key Functions:

- Threat intelligence gathering.
- Real-time monitoring
- Incident response
- Reporting and recommendations

The Open Web Application Security Project (OWASP)

OWASP is a globally recognized nonprofit organization dedicated to improving the security of software and web applications. Founded in

2001, OWASP provides a wealth of free, open-source resources, tools, and best practices for developers, security professionals, and organizations to help them build and maintain secure software.

OWASP Projects:

OWASP Top Ten: A regularly updated list highlighting the top ten most critical security risks to web applications. This list serves as a guideline for developers and security professionals to mitigate common security issues.

OWASP SAMM (Software Assurance Maturity Model): A framework to help organizations formulate and implement a strategy for software security that is tailored to the specific risks facing their organization.

OWASP ASVS (Application Security Verification Standard): A framework for specifying functional and non-functional security controls in web applications and services.

OWASP ZAP (Zed Attack Proxy): An open-source security testing tool for web applications, which helps find security vulnerabilities.

OWASP Cheat Sheets: Comprehensive guides on various security topics providing best practices and recommendations for developers.

OWASP Top Ten

The OWASP Top Ten is one of the most well-known projects, providing a regularly updated list of the most critical web application security risks.

The current list includes:

- Broken Access Control
- Cryptographic Failures
- Injection
- Insecure Design
- Security Misconfiguration
- Vulnerable and Outdated Components

- Identification and Authentication Failures
- OWASP Mobile Top 10 Vulnerabilities
- Software and Data Integrity Failures
- Security Logging and Monitoring Failures
- Server-Side Request Forgery (SSRF)

Network Analyzers

Network analyzers, also known as packet analyzers or protocol analyzers, are tools used to capture, analyze, and diagnose network traffic. They provide insights into the performance, security, and overall health of a network by monitoring the data packets that traverse the network.

Below is an overview of the function, applications and examples of some of the prevalent network analyzers:

Key Functions:

1. **Packet Capturing:**
   - Capture network packets in real-time as they travel across the network.
   - Store packets for offline analysis.

2. **Traffic Analysis:**
   - Examine packet contents to understand data flows and identify protocols used.
   - Analyze traffic patterns to detect anomalies or bottlenecks.

3. **Protocol Decoding:**
   - Decode and display the details of network protocols (e.g., TCP, UDP, HTTP).
   - Provide insights into the protocol-specific operations and issues.

4. **Performance Monitoring:**
   - Measure network performance metrics such as latency, throughput, and packet loss.
   - Identify network performance issues and their root causes.

5. **Security Analysis:**
   - Detect and analyze suspicious or malicious traffic.
   - Monitor for signs of network intrusions or attacks.

6. **Troubleshooting:**
   - Diagnose network problems by examining packet-level data.
   - Identify misconfigurations, hardware failures, or software issues.

Examples of Network Analyzers:

Wireshark is a widely-used open-source network protocol analyzer with a graphical interface that is used for deep inspection of hundreds of protocols, real-time capture and offline analysis, detailed packet analysis, protocol debugging, and security investigations.

TCPdump is a command-line packet analyzer for Unix-like systems that is used for real-time packet capture, filtering capabilities, and basic packet analysis, capturing and analyzing network traffic on the command line.

Windump is a Windows version of TCPdump.

SolarWinds Network Performance Monitor (NPM) is a comprehensive network monitoring tool that provides real-time visibility into continuous network performance and health, network topology mapping, performance metrics, alerts, and reports.

Microsoft Network Monitor (NetMon) (now Microsoft Message Analyzer) captures and analyzes network traffic, decodes various protocols, and is used for analyzing network traffic within Windows networks.

Colasoft Capsa is a network analyzer designed for Windows that provides packet capture, network monitoring, and analysis.

Riverbed SteelCentral Packet Analyzer is a high-performance network analysis tool designed for enterprise networks, advanced packet analysis, performance monitoring, and troubleshooting and is used in large-scale networks for detailed traffic analysis and performance optimization.

Other Advanced Cybersecurity Technologies

Here are a few other cutting-edge cybersecurity technologies that are considered highly advanced:

1. Artificial Intelligence and Machine Learning (AI/ML)

AI and ML are at the forefront of cybersecurity innovation. They are used to develop advanced threat detection and response systems that can identify and mitigate threats in real-time. AI/ML models can analyze vast amounts of data to detect patterns and anomalies that may indicate a cyber-attack.

Use Cases:

- Predictive threat intelligence
- Anomaly detection
- Automated response systems

2. Zero Trust Security

Zero Trust is a security model that assumes that threats could be both external and internal, and therefore, no user or system should be trusted by default. Every access request is verified, and least privilege access principles are applied.

Use Cases:

- Identity and access management (IAM)
- Micro-segmentation
- Continuous authentication and verification

3. Quantum Cryptography

Quantum cryptography uses the principles of quantum mechanics to encrypt data in a way that is theoretically impossible to break.

Quantum key distribution (QKD) is one of the primary methods used in this technology.

Use Cases:

- Secure communication channels
- Advanced encryption methods

4. Blockchain Technology

Blockchain technology provides a decentralized and tamper-proof ledger system. In cybersecurity, it is used to enhance the security of transactions, protect data integrity, and secure identities.

Use Cases:

- Secure data sharing
- Identity verification
- Supply chain security

5. Behavioral Analytics

Behavioral analytics involves monitoring and analyzing user behavior to detect unusual patterns that may indicate a security threat. This approach is particularly effective for identifying insider threats and sophisticated external attacks.

Use Cases:

- User and Entity Behavior Analytics (UEBA)
- Insider threat detection
- Anomaly detection

6. Deception Technology

Deception technology involves creating traps and decoys within a network to lure attackers and detect malicious activities. It helps in identifying and understanding attacker techniques and tactics.

Use Cases:

- Honeypots and honeytokens
- Decoy systems
- Threat intelligence gathering

Comparison

While SOAR is a powerful technology that enhances security operations through integration, automation, and orchestration, it is part of a broader ecosystem of advanced cybersecurity technologies. Each of these technologies addresses different aspects of cybersecurity challenges:

- **SOAR**: Focuses on operational efficiency and response automation.

- **AI/ML**: Provides advanced threat detection and predictive capabilities.

- **XDR**: Offers comprehensive visibility and integrated response across multiple security layers.

- **Zero Trust**: Enforces strict access controls and continuous verification.

- **Quantum Cryptography**: Ensures future-proof encryption.

- **Blockchain**: Secures data integrity and identity verification.

- **Behavioral Analytics**: Detects anomalies and insider threats.

- **Deception Technology**: Captures and analyzes attacker behavior.

Determining the "most advanced" technology depends on the specific needs and context of the organization. Often, a combination of these technologies, integrated into a cohesive cybersecurity strategy, provides the most robust defense against modern cyber threats.

8. Security Information and Event Management (SIEM)

Introduction to SIEM

SIEM systems provide real-time analysis of security alerts generated by applications and network hardware. They collect, analyze, and report on security data from across an organization's IT environment.

Functions of SIEM

- **Data aggregation:** Collects data from various sources.
- **Correlation:** Identifies relationships between different events.
- **Alerting:** Notifies security teams of potential threats.
- **Dashboards:** Visual representations of security data.
- **Compliance:** Helps meet regulatory requirements.

Examples of SIEM

Security Information and Event Management (SIEM) systems are essential tools for managing and analyzing security information and events in real-time. They help organizations identify and respond to potential threats quickly. Here are some examples of popular SIEM solutions:

- Splunk Enterprise Security
- IBM QRadar
- Sequretek Percept (XDR+NG SIEM)
- ArchSight Enterprise Security Manager (ESM)
- LogRythm NextGen SIEM
- McAfee Enterprise Security manager

- Microsoft Azure Sentinel
- Google Chronicle SIEM
- Amazon GuardDuty (threat detection)
- Amazon AWS Inspector (automated security assessment)

SIEM Integration with XDR

The landscape of cybersecurity is evolving rapidly, driven by the increasing complexity and frequency of cyber threats. Traditional security measures are no longer sufficient to protect against sophisticated attacks. Extended Detection and Response (XDR) and Security Information and Event Management (SIEM) are two technologies at the forefront of modern cybersecurity. Their integration, powered by artificial intelligence (AI), promises to enhance and strengthen security operations significantly.

Combining SIEM with XDR provides comprehensive threat detection and response capabilities by leveraging the data aggregation and correlation strengths of SIEM with the advanced detection and automated response features of XDR.

One of the leading cybersecurity platforms in this category is Sequretek's AI powered XDR+NG SIEM platform called "Percept".

9. Incident Response and Management (IRM)

In today's interconnected digital landscape, organizations face a constant barrage of cyber threats ranging from malware attacks to data breaches and ransomware incidents. Incident Response and Management (IRM) is the structured approach organizations adopt to handle these security breaches promptly and effectively. It involves:

Incident Response Plan

An incident response plan is a set of instructions to help IT staff detect, respond to, and recover from network security incidents. These incidents include cyberattacks, data breaches, and system failures.

Forensics and Investigation

Cyber forensics involves analyzing digital evidence to understand the nature of an incident, identify the perpetrators, and prevent future attacks. This includes collecting, preserving, and analyzing data from compromised systems.

Recovery and Lessons Learned

After addressing an incident, organizations must recover and restore normal operations. This involves removing malware, restoring data from backups, and improving security measures to prevent future incidents. Learning from incidents helps organizations strengthen their security posture.

Key Components of Incident Response

1. Preparation:

- **Risk Assessment:** Organizations begin by identifying and prioritizing potential risks and vulnerabilities.
- **Planning:** Comprehensive incident response plans (IRPs) are developed, outlining roles, responsibilities, and predefined steps for different types of incidents.
- **Training and Drills:** Regular training sessions and simulated exercises ensure that the response team is well-prepared to handle real-world incidents.

2. Detection and Reporting:

- **Monitoring Systems:** Continuous monitoring of network traffic, logs, and system behaviors helps in early detection of anomalies.
- **Alerting Mechanisms:** Automated alerts and manual monitoring ensure that suspicious activities are promptly reported to the response team.

3. Response and Mitigation:

- **Containment:** Isolating affected systems or networks to prevent further damage.
- **Eradication:** Removing the root cause of the incident, such as malware or unauthorized access.
- **Recovery:** Restoring affected systems and data from backups while ensuring their integrity.

4. Investigation and Analysis:

- **Forensic Analysis:** Examining the incident to understand its scope, impact, and methods used by attackers.
- **Attribution:** Identifying the source of the attack or breach to prevent future occurrences.

5. **Post-Incident Activity:**

- **Documentation:** Detailed documentation of the incident, including actions taken and lessons learned.
- **Review and Improvement:** Conducting post-mortem reviews to identify weaknesses in the IRP and implementing necessary improvements.

Example of IRM Application

Let's consider a hypothetical scenario where a large financial institution detects unauthorized access to its customer database:

Detection and Initial Response:

- The organization's monitoring system flags unusual database queries.
- The incident response team is alerted, and immediate containment measures are implemented by isolating the compromised servers.

Investigation and Recovery:

- Forensic experts analyze the database logs to determine the extent of data accessed.
- Data affected by the breach is identified, and unaffected data is restored from recent backups.
- Security patches are applied to the database software to prevent similar incidents in the future.

Post-Incident Review:

- A comprehensive review identifies gaps in the organization's access control policies.
- Employee training programs are enhanced to raise awareness about phishing attacks, which were the initial vector of the breach.
- The incident response plan is updated to include specific procedures for database breaches and refined communication protocols.

Incident Response and Management is not just about reacting to security breaches but also about proactive preparation and continuous improvement. By adopting a structured approach that integrates detection, response, mitigation, and learning, organizations can effectively minimize the impact of cyber incidents while strengthening their overall cybersecurity resilience. In an increasingly digital world, IRM remains an essential pillar of a robust cybersecurity strategy, ensuring that organizations can navigate and mitigate the evolving landscape of cyber threats effectively.

10. Enterprise-wide Threat Detection and Response Landscape

Cybersecurity is a complex and multifaceted domain, brimming with a myriad of concepts, tools, and specialized terminology that can often seem overwhelming. To simplify and clarify how these various elements interconnect, let's explore how these tools collaborate within an enterprise-wide threat detection and response landscape. Understanding their integrated functions and interactions will provide a clearer picture of how they collectively enhance an organization's security posture.

In an integrated enterprise-wide threat detection and response landscape, the process can be categorized into eight phases:

- **Data Collection and Correlation:** SIEM collects data from EDR, NTDR, PAM, and other sources. UEBA and XDR correlate this data to provide a unified view of security events.

- **Continuous Monitoring:** SOC uses SIEM, XDR, and NTDR for continuous monitoring and real-time threat detection.

- **Automated Response:** SOAR automates responses to detected threats, coordinating actions across EDR, PAM, and other tools.

- **Proactive Threat Hunting:** Threat hunters leverage data from EDR, SIEM, and threat intelligence to identify and mitigate advanced threats.

- **Access Controls:** IAG, PAM, and Zero Trust enforce strict access controls, ensuring only authorized users and devices can access sensitive resources.

- **Incident Response:** IDR and MDR provide structured incident response, using data from SIEM, EDR, and XDR to contain and remediate threats.

- **Continuous Improvement:** OWASP guidelines and threat intelligence from MTIR ensure that the security posture evolves to meet new challenges.

- **Compliance and Governance:** IAG and SIEM support compliance with regulatory requirements, providing audit trails and reporting capabilities.

The integration and proper sequencing of various cybersecurity and IT management tools and techniques are crucial for establishing a robust security posture. Below is a detailed breakdown of these tools and how they work together, organized in a logical sequence that illustrates their interdependencies and collaborative functionalities:

1. Checkpoints

Function: Act as control points in the network to enforce security policies and monitor traffic.

Integration: Establish the first line of defense, setting up firewall rules, intrusion prevention systems (IPS), and other security measures.

2. Network Analyzers

Function: Monitor network traffic to identify anomalies, potential intrusions, and performance issues.

Integration: Provide visibility into network activities, essential for detecting threats and understanding traffic patterns.

3. Network Threat Detection and Response (NTDR)

Function: Detect and respond to threats at the network level, often using AI and machine learning.

Integration: Build on insights from network analyzers to identify and mitigate threats before they impact the system.

4. Identity Threat Detection and Response (ITDR)

Function: Monitor and respond to identity-related threats, such as compromised credentials.

Integration: Complement NTDR by focusing on the user level, ensuring that identity-based threats are identified and managed.

5. Security Information and Event Management (SIEM)

Function: Collect, correlate, and analyze security event data from various sources to provide a centralized view of security incidents.

Integration: Aggregate logs and event data from NTDR, ITDR, EDR, and other sources to identify patterns and provide actionable insights.

6. Endpoint Detection and Response (EDR)

Function: Monitor and respond to threats at endpoints (e.g., computers, mobile devices).

Integration: Work with NTDR, ITDR, and SIEM to provide comprehensive threat detection across network and endpoints.

7. Extended Detection and Response (XDR)

Function: Integrate data from multiple security layers (network, endpoint, server) to provide a unified response.

Integration: Enhance the effectiveness of NTDR, ITDR, EDR, and SIEM by correlating data from various sources for better threat visibility and response.

8. User and Entity Behavior Analytics (UEBA)

Function: Analyze user and entity behavior to identify anomalies that may indicate insider threats or compromised accounts.

Integration: Provide behavioral context to NTDR, ITDR, EDR, and SIEM, improving the detection of sophisticated threats.

9. Threat Hunter

Function: Proactively search for threats within the network and systems that may have evaded automated defenses.

Integration: Collaborate with NTDR, ITDR, EDR, XDR, and SIEM to hunt for threats using insights from these systems.

10. Privileged Access Management (PAM)

Function: Control and monitor privileged accounts to prevent misuse.

Integration: Strengthen ITDR by managing and securing privileged access, reducing the risk of identity-based attacks.

11. Identity and Access Governance (IAG)

Function: Ensure that user access rights are appropriate and comply with policies.

Integration: Support PAM and ITDR by providing governance and oversight of access management.

12. OWASP Top 10

Function: Provide a list of the most critical web application security risks.

Integration: Guide the development and security testing of applications to mitigate common vulnerabilities, complementing broader security efforts.

13. MITRE ATT&CK Framework

Function: Provide a comprehensive matrix of tactics and techniques used by adversaries.

Integration: Serve as a reference for understanding and defending against common attack patterns, informing the configurations of NTDR, EDR, XDR, and SIEM systems.

14. Security Orchestration, Automation, and Response (SOAR)

Function: Automate and coordinate security operations, including incident response.

Integration: Use data from NTDR, EDR, XDR, SIEM, and other sources to automate responses, reducing response times and improving efficiency.

15. Managed Detection and Response (MDR)

Function: Provide outsourced monitoring and response capabilities.

Integration: Extend the capabilities of in-house teams by offering expert threat detection and response services.

16. Incident Detection and Response (IDR)

Function: Detect and respond to security incidents.

Integration: Act as the operational framework for handling incidents, leveraging tools like SOAR, MDR, EDR, and SIEM for effective management.

17. Disaster Recovery and Incident Response

Function: Plan and execute recovery procedures after a security incident or disaster.

Integration: Ensure business continuity by having well-defined processes for recovering from incidents, informed by insights from IDR, SOAR, and SIEM.

This is how the sequence of this interaction looks like:

- **Initial Defense and Monitoring**: Checkpoints and Network Analyzers establish and monitor network defenses.

- **Detection and Response Integration**: NTDR, ITDR, and SIEM provide detection and response capabilities at various levels (network, identity, centralized event management).

- **Endpoint and Extended Detection**: EDR and XDR enhance detection at endpoints and across multiple layers.

- **Behavioral Analysis and Threat Hunting**: UEBA and Threat Hunter improve detection with behavioral insights and proactive threat searches.

- **Access Control and Governance**: PAM and IAG manage and govern access, reducing the risk of identity-based attacks.

- **Application Security**: OWASP Top 10 guides secure application development and testing.

- **Attack Understanding**: MTIR informs security configurations and threat understanding.

- **Automation and Coordination**: SOAR automates and coordinates responses, improving efficiency.

- **Outsourced Support**: MDR offers additional support and expertise.

- **Incident Management**: IDR handles incidents, while Disaster Recovery ensures business continuity.

11. Cybersecurity Best Practices

In an era where digital transformation is integral to business success, cybersecurity has become a paramount concern for organizations of all sizes. Cyber threats are continually evolving, making it imperative for businesses and individuals to adopt robust cybersecurity practices. The guide below outlines key cybersecurity best practices that can help protect your digital assets from malicious actors.

1. User Training and Awareness

Training employees on cybersecurity best practices is crucial for protecting an organization from threats. This includes recognizing phishing attempts, using strong passwords, and following company security policies. Employees training may include:

Security Awareness Training: Conduct regular training sessions to educate employees about cybersecurity risks, phishing attacks, and safe online practices.

Simulated Phishing Exercises: Test employee awareness with simulated phishing campaigns to reinforce training.

Policy Adherence: Ensure all staff are aware of and adhere to the organization's security policies and procedures.

2. Implement Strong Password Policies

Implementing strong password policies ensures that passwords are difficult to guess or crack. This includes using a combination of letters, numbers, and special characters, and changing passwords regularly.

Use Complex Passwords: Ensure passwords are long and include a mix of upper-case and lower-case letters, numbers, and special characters.

Regular Password Updates: Mandate periodic password changes to minimize the risk of compromised credentials.

Avoid Reuse: Do not reuse passwords across different accounts to prevent a breach in one service from compromising others.

3. Enable Multi-Factor Authentication (MFA)

Add Extra Layers: Require an additional verification step beyond the password, such as a text message code, authenticator app, or biometric scan.

Reduce Risk: MFA significantly reduces the chances of unauthorized access even if passwords are compromised.

4. Regularly Update and Patch Systems

Stay Current: Keep all operating systems, applications, and software up to date with the latest patches and updates.

Automate Where Possible: Use automated tools to manage and deploy updates promptly.

Address Vulnerabilities: Prioritize patching critical vulnerabilities that could be exploited by cybercriminals.

5. Regular Audits and Assessments

Conducting regular security audits and assessments helps identify vulnerabilities and ensure that security measures are effective. This includes reviewing access controls, monitoring network traffic, and testing security protocols. This may include:

Vulnerability Assessments: Periodically evaluate systems and networks for vulnerabilities.

Penetration Testing: Engage ethical hackers to conduct penetration tests and identify potential security weaknesses.

Compliance Checks: Ensure adherence to industry standards and regulatory requirements through regular compliance audits.

6. Use Firewalls and Antivirus Software

Network Security: Deploy firewalls to protect the network perimeter and prevent unauthorized access.

Endpoint Protection: Install and maintain reliable antivirus software on all devices to detect and remove malware.

Regular Scans: Conduct regular scans to identify and mitigate potential threats.

7. Secure Remote Work

VPN Usage: Require employees to use Virtual Private Networks (VPNs) when accessing company resources remotely.

Secure Connections: Ensure remote connections are encrypted to protect data in transit.

Device Management: Implement Mobile Device Management (MDM) solutions to enforce security policies on remote devices.

8. Backup Data Regularly

Frequent Backups: Perform regular backups of critical data to ensure it can be restored in the event of a cyber incident.

Offsite Storage: Store backups in secure, offsite locations to protect against physical damage or theft.

Test Restorations: Regularly test backup restorations to ensure data can be successfully recovered.

9. Implement Least Privilege Access

Restrict Permissions: Grant users the minimum level of access necessary to perform their jobs.

Role-Based Access Control: Use role-based access control (RBAC) to manage permissions based on job roles.

Review Access Regularly: Periodically review and adjust access permissions as needed.

10. Develop and Enforce a Robust Incident Response Plan

Preparation: Establish a comprehensive incident response plan detailing steps to take in the event of a cybersecurity incident.

Team Formation: Designate an incident response team with clearly defined roles and responsibilities.

Drill and Improve: Regularly conduct incident response drills to ensure the team is prepared and identify areas for improvement.

11. Risk Response, Mitigation, and Control

Managing cybersecurity risks involves several strategies:

Risk Response: Determining how to handle identified risks (e.g., accept, avoid, transfer).

Mitigation: Implementing measures to reduce the impact of risks.

Control: Establishing policies, procedures, and technologies to enforce security.

12. Ten Rules of Operational Security (OpSec)

Operational Security, commonly known as OpSec, is a critical practice in safeguarding information and ensuring that sensitive data is protected from adversaries. Originally developed by the military, OpSec is now widely used in corporate environments to prevent data breaches, protect intellectual property, and maintain overall security.

Here are ten essential rules of OpSec that organizations and individuals should follow to enhance their security posture.

1. **Identify Critical Information** The first step in OpSec is to identify what information needs to be protected. This includes intellectual property, proprietary data, personal information, and any other sensitive material. By understanding what constitutes critical information, organizations can better focus their security efforts.

2. **Analyze Threats** Once critical information is identified, the next step is to analyze potential threats. This involves understanding who might want to access the information, why they want it, and how they might go about obtaining it. This can include competitors, cybercriminals, or even disgruntled employees.

3. **Assess Vulnerabilities** Assessing vulnerabilities involves identifying weaknesses in the current security setup that could be exploited by adversaries. This could be anything from outdated software, weak passwords, unsecured networks, or insufficient access controls.

4. **Implement Countermeasures** To mitigate identified vulnerabilities, appropriate countermeasures must be put in place. These can include technical solutions like firewalls, encryption, and multi-factor authentication, as well as procedural measures such as regular audits and employee training.

5. **Limit Information Dissemination** A fundamental principle of OpSec is the "need-to-know" basis. Information should only be shared with individuals who require it to perform their

duties. Limiting the dissemination of critical information reduces the risk of accidental leaks or intentional breaches.

6. **Monitor and Review Security** is not a set-and-forget task. Continuous monitoring and regular reviews are essential to ensure that security measures are effective and up-to-date. This includes monitoring network traffic, conducting security audits, and reviewing access logs.

7. **Educate and Train Employees** Human error is one of the biggest risks to OpSec. Regular training and education for employees on security best practices, recognizing phishing attempts, and the importance of following security protocols can significantly enhance overall security.

8. **Secure Physical Access** Physical security is just as important as digital security. Access to buildings, offices, and data centers should be controlled and monitored. This can include measures such as key cards, biometric scanners, security cameras, and visitor logs.

9. **Use Strong Authentication Methods** Passwords alone are often not enough to secure critical information. Implementing strong authentication methods, such as multi-factor authentication (MFA), can add an extra layer of security by requiring additional verification steps before access is granted.

10. **Develop and Enforce Policies** Clear, enforceable policies are essential for effective OpSec. These policies should outline acceptable use, data handling procedures, incident response plans, and disciplinary measures for non-compliance. Ensuring that all employees are aware of and adhere to these policies is crucial for maintaining a secure environment.

Operational Security is an ongoing process that requires vigilance, adaptability, and a proactive approach. By following these ten rules, organizations can significantly enhance their security posture, protect critical information, and reduce the risk of security breaches. In today's digital landscape, robust OpSec practices are not just a necessity but a fundamental component of any comprehensive security strategy.

12. Tracking and Privacy Concerns

How We Are Tracked Online

Various methods are used to track online activities:

- **Cookies:** Small files stored on your device that track browsing history.

- **IP addresses:** Identifies your device's location on the internet.

- **Browser fingerprints:** Collects information about your browser settings and device.

- **Tracking pixels:** Invisible images that track email and web page interactions.

- **Social media:** Platforms collect data based on interactions and content sharing.

SSD Forensics

SSD Forensics involves analyzing solid-state drives (SSDs) to uncover digital evidence. Unlike traditional hard drives, SSDs use flash memory and have unique challenges:

- **Wear leveling:** Distributes data evenly across the drive, complicating data retrieval.

- **TRIM command:** Automatically deletes data, making it harder to recover deleted files.

- **Volatility:** SSDs retain data differently, requiring specialized tools and techniques for forensic analysis.

Door Locks

Door Locks: Physical security measures to control access to buildings and rooms:

- **Electronic locks:** Use key cards or fobs.
- **Biometric locks:** Use fingerprints or other biometric data
- **Smart locks:** Controlled via smartphones or other devices.

Access Badge Cloning

The practice of duplicating access badges to gain unauthorized entry:

- **Cloning devices:** Tools that read and duplicate RFID or NFC signals from access badges.
- **Preventive measures:** Using encrypted and tamper-resistant badges.

13. Interoperability Issues

Challenges with Multiple Devices

As the number of connected devices grows, ensuring compatibility and interoperability between different systems becomes increasingly challenging. Diverse operating systems, hardware configurations, and communication protocols can create security vulnerabilities.

Solutions for Interoperability

To address these challenges, organizations can implement standardized protocols, use middleware solutions, and invest in comprehensive testing and validation processes to ensure that all devices and systems work seamlessly together while maintaining security.

Understanding the fundamental concepts of cybersecurity is crucial for navigating the complexities of the digital age. From recognizing different types of cyber threats to implementing best practices and staying informed about future trends, individuals and organizations can better protect themselves against cyberattacks. By prioritizing cybersecurity and adopting a proactive approach, we can build a safer digital environment for everyone.

PART II

DIGITAL DEFENSE GUIDE FOR BUSINESS LEADERS AND BOARD DIRECTORS

14. Introduction to Cybersecurity for Board Directors

Importance of Cybersecurity in Corporate Governance

In today's digital age, cybersecurity has become a critical component of corporate governance. The proliferation of digital technologies, cloud computing, and interconnected systems has exposed organizations to a myriad of cyber threats. These threats range from data breaches and ransomware attacks to sophisticated state-sponsored cyber espionage. The consequences of a successful cyberattack can be devastating, resulting in financial losses, reputational damage, legal liabilities, and operational disruptions.

Board directors play a pivotal role in ensuring that their organizations are adequately protected against these cyber threats. As stewards of the company, directors have a fiduciary duty to safeguard the organization's assets, which increasingly include digital information and IT infrastructure. Cybersecurity is not just a technical issue but a business imperative that requires strategic oversight and governance at the highest levels of the organization.

The Evolving Threat Landscape

The cybersecurity landscape is constantly evolving, with new threats emerging at an alarming rate. Cybercriminals are becoming more sophisticated, employing advanced tactics such as social engineering, phishing, and zero-day exploits. Additionally, the rise of the Internet of Things (IoT), artificial intelligence (AI), and machine learning has introduced new vulnerabilities and attack vectors.

Several key trends highlight the evolving threat landscape:

1. **Increased Frequency and Severity of Cyber Attacks**: Cyber-attacks are becoming more frequent and severe, with

high-profile incidents making headlines regularly. These attacks can target any organization, regardless of size or industry, underscoring the universal nature of the threat.

2. **Ransomware and Malware**: Ransomware attacks have surged, with cybercriminals encrypting an organization's data and demanding a ransom for its release. Malware, including viruses, worms, and trojans, continues to be a significant threat, often serving as the initial point of entry for more extensive attacks.

3. **Phishing and Social Engineering**: Phishing attacks, where attackers deceive individuals into divulging sensitive information, remain prevalent. Social engineering tactics, which exploit human psychology to manipulate individuals into performing actions or divulging confidential information, are also on the rise.

4. **State-Sponsored Attacks**: Nation-states are increasingly engaging in cyber espionage and cyber warfare, targeting critical infrastructure, government agencies, and private sector organizations. These attacks are often highly sophisticated and well-funded.

5. **Supply Chain Vulnerabilities**: The interconnected nature of modern supply chains introduces vulnerabilities that can be exploited by cyber attackers. Compromising a single supplier can provide access to multiple organizations within the supply chain.

Given this dynamic and complex threat environment, it is essential for board directors to stay informed about the latest trends and developments in cybersecurity. This knowledge enables directors to ask the right questions, understand the potential impact of cyber threats on the organization, and ensure that appropriate measures are in place to mitigate these risks.

The Role of Board Directors

Board directors are responsible for overseeing the overall governance and strategic direction of the organization. In the context of cybersecurity, this includes:

1. **Setting the Tone at the Top**: Board directors must emphasize the importance of cybersecurity as a critical aspect of the organization's culture and values. This involves promoting a security-first mindset and encouraging all employees to take cybersecurity seriously.

2. **Ensuring Adequate Resources**: Directors must ensure that the organization allocates sufficient resources—financial, technical, and human—to cybersecurity initiatives. This includes investing in advanced security technologies, hiring skilled cybersecurity professionals, and providing ongoing training and awareness programs.

3. **Risk Oversight**: Directors should oversee the organization's cybersecurity risk management practices, ensuring that robust risk assessment and mitigation strategies are in place. This involves regularly reviewing cybersecurity policies, procedures, and controls, as well as understanding the potential impact of cyber risks on the organization's strategic objectives.

4. **Monitoring and Reporting**: Directors must ensure that there are effective mechanisms for monitoring and reporting on cybersecurity risks and incidents. This includes receiving regular updates from the Chief Information Security Officer (CISO) or equivalent, and understanding key cybersecurity metrics and indicators.

5. **Incident Response and Crisis Management**: Directors play a crucial role in overseeing the organization's incident response and crisis management capabilities. This includes ensuring that there are well-defined incident response plans in place, and that the organization is prepared to respond swiftly and effectively to cyber incidents.

Cybersecurity is a vital aspect of corporate governance that requires active and informed oversight by board directors. By understanding the evolving threat landscape and fulfilling their responsibilities in cybersecurity governance, directors can help protect their organizations from cyber threats and ensure long-term resilience and success.

15. Board Directors' Responsibilities in Cybersecurity

Fiduciary Duties and Cybersecurity

Board directors have a fiduciary duty to act in the best interests of the company and its shareholders. This duty encompasses a broad range of responsibilities, including the oversight of cybersecurity risks. Directors must ensure that the organization has effective cybersecurity measures in place to protect its assets, data, and reputation. Failing to adequately address cybersecurity can result in significant financial losses, legal liabilities, and damage to the company's brand.

Directors' fiduciary duties in the context of cybersecurity include:

1. **Duty of Care**: Directors must make informed and prudent decisions regarding the organization's cybersecurity posture. This involves staying informed about the latest cybersecurity threats, understanding the organization's current security measures, and ensuring that adequate resources are allocated to cybersecurity initiatives.

2. **Duty of Loyalty**: Directors must prioritize the interests of the company and its shareholders when making decisions about cybersecurity. This means avoiding conflicts of interest and ensuring that cybersecurity policies and practices align with the overall strategic goals of the organization.

3. **Duty of Oversight**: Directors are responsible for overseeing the implementation and effectiveness of the organization's cybersecurity program. This includes regularly reviewing cybersecurity policies, procedures, and controls, and holding management accountable for their execution.

Legal and Regulatory Obligations

Organizations are subject to various legal and regulatory requirements related to cybersecurity. Board directors must ensure that the company complies with these requirements to avoid legal penalties and reputational damage. Key regulatory frameworks and laws that directors should be aware of include:

1. **SEC's New Cybersecurity Disclosure Rule:** Codified under Regulation S-K, Item 106 (risk management and governance disclosure) and Item 1.05 of Form 8-K (for incident reporting) require detailed disclosures on how companies manage and govern cybersecurity risks, and mandate the timely reporting of material cybersecurity incidents (within 4 business days). The rules are designed to provide consistent and useful information to investors about cybersecurity threats and the measures companies take to mitigate these risks.

   Below are the key points of this new regulations:

   - **Incident Reporting:** Public companies must report material cybersecurity incidents on a new Form 8-K item (for domestic issuers) or Form 6-K (for foreign private issuers). These disclosures are required to be made without "unreasonable delay" once a materiality assessment is completed. Companies must also provide updates on the incident as new information becomes available, within four business days of determining such information.

   - **Risk Management and Governance Disclosures:** Companies are required to include detailed information on their processes for assessing, identifying, and managing cybersecurity risks in their annual reports (Forms 10-K and 20-F). This includes how these processes are integrated into the overall risk management framework, the involvement of third parties, and the impact of previous cybersecurity incidents on the company's business strategy, operations, and financial condition.

- **Board Oversight:** Companies must describe the board's role in overseeing cybersecurity risks, including identifying the board committees responsible and the processes for keeping the board informed about cybersecurity issues. This is to ensure that there is adequate oversight at the highest levels of the organization

- **Structured Data Requirements (Inline XBRL Tagging):** Companies are required to tag the disclosures in Inline XBRL format, with a staggered compliance date of one year after the initial compliance date of the related disclosure requirement. This aims to facilitate better data analysis and comparability for investors

    Compliance Dates:

    - Large companies must comply with the incident disclosure requirements starting December 18, 2023, or 90 days after the rules are published in the Federal Register, whichever is later.

    - Smaller reporting companies have an extended compliance period until June 15, 2024, or 270 days after the rules are published

2. **General Data Protection Regulation (GDPR):** This European Union regulation imposes strict requirements on organizations that process personal data of EU residents. Directors must ensure that the organization complies with GDPR requirements, including data protection principles, individual rights, and breach notification obligations.

3. **Health Insurance Portability and Accountability Act (HIPAA):** This U.S. law requires healthcare organizations to protect the privacy and security of patients' health information. Directors must ensure that the organization implements appropriate safeguards to protect health data and complies with HIPAA regulations.

4. **Sarbanes-Oxley Act (SOX):** This U.S. law mandates that publicly traded companies implement internal controls to

ensure the accuracy and reliability of financial reporting. Directors must ensure that cybersecurity controls are integrated into the organization's overall internal control framework.

5. **Payment Card Industry Data Security Standard (PCI DSS)**: This set of security standards applies to organizations that process credit card payments. Directors must ensure that the organization complies with PCI DSS requirements to protect payment card data.

6. **Gramm-Leach-Bliley Act (GLBA)**: Gramm-Leach Bliley Act is enforced by FTC and federal banking regulators and requires the financial institutions to safeguard customer data

7. **Defense Federal Acquisition Regulation Supplement (DoD - DFARS) Requirements**: Companies contracting with the DoD must adhere to specific cybersecurity standards. Non-compliance can lead to the loss of current and future contracts, along with potential financial penalties.

8. **Other Regulations**: In addition to federal regulations, organizations may be subject to state and local cybersecurity laws. Directors must ensure that the organization is aware of and complies with all applicable regulations. Some of the examples are California Consumer Privacy Act (CCPA), New York SHIELD Act, Computer Fraud and Abuse Act (CFAA), Financial Regulatory Authority (FINRA) cybersecurity regulations for member firms, Family Educational Rights and Privacy Act (FERPA), North American Electric Reliability Corporation's Critical Infrastructure Protection Standards (NERC CIP) etc.

Ethical Considerations

Beyond legal and regulatory obligations, directors have an ethical responsibility to protect the privacy and security of their stakeholders' information. This includes employees, customers, partners, and investors. Ethical considerations in cybersecurity governance include:

1. **Transparency**: Directors should promote transparency in the organization's cybersecurity practices. This involves openly communicating cybersecurity risks and incidents to stakeholders and being honest about the organization's efforts to mitigate these risks.

2. **Accountability**: Directors must hold themselves and the organization accountable for cybersecurity performance. This includes setting clear expectations for management, regularly reviewing cybersecurity metrics, and taking corrective actions when necessary.

3. **Fairness**: Directors should ensure that the organization's cybersecurity policies and practices are fair and non-discriminatory. This includes protecting all stakeholders' information equally and avoiding practices that could disproportionately impact certain groups.

Setting the Tone at the Top

Board directors play a crucial role in setting the tone for cybersecurity within the organization. By demonstrating a commitment to cybersecurity, directors can influence the entire organization to prioritize and take responsibility for security. Key actions directors can take to set the tone at the top include:

1. **Communicating the Importance of Cybersecurity**: Directors should regularly communicate the importance of cybersecurity to employees, management, and stakeholders. This can be done through speeches, internal communications, and public statements.

2. **Leading by Example**: Directors should model good cybersecurity behavior by following best practices, such as using strong passwords, enabling multi-factor authentication, and participating in cybersecurity training.

3. **Promoting a Security-First Culture**: Directors should encourage a culture where cybersecurity is seen as everyone's responsibility. This involves fostering open communication about security issues, recognizing and rewarding good security

practices, and ensuring that employees feel empowered to report security concerns.

Ensuring Adequate Resources

Directors must ensure that the organization allocates sufficient resources to cybersecurity initiatives. This includes financial, technical, and human resources. Key considerations include:

1. **Budgeting for Cybersecurity**: Directors should work with management to ensure that the organization has a dedicated cybersecurity budget that covers necessary tools, technologies, and personnel.

2. **Hiring and Retaining Cybersecurity Talent**: Directors should support efforts to hire and retain skilled cybersecurity professionals. This may involve offering competitive salaries, providing ongoing training and development opportunities, and creating a positive work environment.

3. **Investing in Technology and Infrastructure**: Directors should ensure that the organization invests in advanced cybersecurity technologies and infrastructure. This includes firewalls, intrusion detection/prevention systems, encryption, and other security tools.

Risk Oversight

Directors are responsible for overseeing the organization's cybersecurity risk management practices. This involves understanding the organization's risk profile, identifying potential threats, and ensuring that appropriate mitigation strategies are in place. Key actions include:

1. **Conducting Regular Risk Assessments**: Directors should ensure that the organization conducts regular risk assessments to identify and evaluate cybersecurity threats. This involves assessing the likelihood and impact of potential incidents and prioritizing risks based on their severity.

2. **Developing a Risk Management Framework**: Directors should work with management to develop a comprehensive risk management framework that includes policies, procedures, and controls for mitigating cybersecurity risks.
3. **Monitoring and Reviewing Risks**: Directors should regularly monitor and review the organization's cybersecurity risks. This involves receiving regular updates from the Chief Information Security Officer (CISO) or equivalent, and reviewing key risk indicators and metrics.

Monitoring and Reporting

Effective monitoring and reporting mechanisms are essential for ensuring that the organization's cybersecurity program is functioning as intended. Directors should:

1. **Establish Clear Reporting Lines**: Directors should ensure that there are clear reporting lines for cybersecurity issues. This includes designating a senior executive, such as the CISO, to report directly to the board on cybersecurity matters.

2. **Review Cybersecurity Metrics**: Directors should regularly review key cybersecurity metrics, such as the number of incidents, response times, and the effectiveness of security controls. This helps directors assess the organization's cybersecurity performance and identify areas for improvement.

3. **Conduct Regular Audits**: Directors should ensure that the organization conducts regular audits of its cybersecurity practices. This includes internal audits, as well as third-party assessments, to verify compliance with policies and identify potential vulnerabilities.

Incident Response and Crisis Management

Directors play a crucial role in overseeing the organization's incident response and crisis management capabilities. This involves ensuring that the organization is prepared to respond swiftly and effectively to cyber incidents. Key actions include:

1. **Developing Incident Response Plans**: Directors should work with management to develop comprehensive incident response plans that outline the steps to be taken in the event of a cybersecurity incident. This includes roles and responsibilities, communication protocols, and escalation procedures.

2. **Conducting Incident Response Drills**: Directors should ensure that the organization conducts regular incident response drills to test the effectiveness of its plans and identify areas for improvement.

3. **Managing Crises**: In the event of a major cyber incident, directors should play an active role in managing the crisis. This includes coordinating with management, communicating with stakeholders, and overseeing the implementation of recovery efforts.

Board directors have a critical role in overseeing and guiding their organization's cybersecurity efforts. By fulfilling their fiduciary duties, understanding legal and regulatory obligations, promoting ethical practices, and ensuring adequate resources and risk management, directors can help protect their organizations from cyber threats and ensure long-term resilience and success.

16. Risk Assessment and Management

Risk assessment and management are critical components of an effective cybersecurity strategy. Board directors must ensure that the organization systematically identifies, evaluates, and mitigates cyber risks. The process typically involves the following steps:

1. **Identify Assets**: Determine which assets are most critical to the organization's operations and success. This includes data, systems, applications, and infrastructure.

2. **Identify Threats**: Identify potential cyber threats that could impact the organization. This includes both external threats (e.g., hackers, malware) and internal threats (e.g., insider threats, human error).

3. **Identify Vulnerabilities**: Assess the organization's systems and processes to identify vulnerabilities that could be exploited by threats. This includes software vulnerabilities, misconfigurations, and weak security practices.

4. **Assess Risk**: Evaluate the likelihood and potential impact of identified threats exploiting vulnerabilities. This involves considering factors such as the threat actor's capabilities, the effectiveness of existing controls, and the potential consequences of a successful attack.

5. **Develop Risk Mitigation Strategies**: Implement measures to reduce the likelihood and impact of cyber risks. This includes technical controls (e.g., firewalls, encryption), procedural controls (e.g., policies, training), and physical controls (e.g., access restrictions, surveillance).

6. **Monitor and Review**: Continuously monitor the organization's cybersecurity posture and review risk management practices. This involves regular audits, vulnerability assessments, and updates to risk mitigation

strategies based on emerging threats and changes in the organization's environment.

Impact of Cyber Incidents on Business Continuity and Reputation

Cyber incidents can have far-reaching consequences for an organization's business continuity and reputation. Board directors must understand these potential impacts to ensure effective risk management and incident response planning.

1. **Financial Loss**: Cyber incidents can result in significant financial losses due to business disruption, data loss, regulatory fines, legal fees, and ransom payments. For example, a ransomware attack can halt operations, leading to lost revenue and increased recovery costs.

2. **Operational Disruption**: Cyber incidents can disrupt critical business processes and operations. This can affect the availability of services, productivity, and the ability to meet customer demands. For instance, a DDoS attack can render a company's website or online services inaccessible.

3. **Legal Liabilities**: Data breaches can compromise sensitive information, including personal data, intellectual property, and financial records. This can lead to legal liabilities, regulatory penalties, and loss of customer trust. For example, a breach of customer data can result in fines under regulations such as GDPR or HIPAA.

4. **Reputational Damage**: Cyber incidents can damage an organization's reputation and erode stakeholder trust. Customers, investors, and partners may lose confidence in the organization's ability to protect their information and maintain secure operations. Rebuilding a damaged reputation can take significant time and resources.

5. **Regulatory and Legal Consequences**: Organizations may face regulatory scrutiny and legal action following a cyber incident. Non-compliance with data protection and cybersecurity regulations can result in fines, sanctions, and

lawsuits. Directors must ensure that the organization adheres to applicable laws and regulations to mitigate these risks.

Strategies for Effective Risk Management

Board directors must ensure that the organization adopts comprehensive strategies to manage cyber risks effectively. Key strategies include:

1. **Implementing a Cybersecurity Framework**: Adopting a recognized cybersecurity framework, such as the NIST Cybersecurity Framework or ISO/IEC 27001, provides a structured approach to managing cyber risks. These frameworks offer guidelines for identifying, protecting, detecting, responding to, and recovering from cyber threats.

2. **Conducting Regular Risk Assessments**: Regular risk assessments help identify new threats and vulnerabilities and evaluate the effectiveness of existing controls. Directors should ensure that risk assessments are conducted periodically and whenever significant changes occur in the organization's environment.

3. **Developing Incident Response Plans**: Comprehensive incident response plans outline the steps to be taken in the event of a cyber incident. These plans should include roles and responsibilities, communication protocols, and procedures for containment, eradication, and recovery. Regular testing and updates ensure that the plans remain effective.

4. **Enhancing Security Awareness and Training**: Human error is a common cause of cyber incidents. Directors should ensure that employees receive regular training on cybersecurity best practices, including recognizing phishing attempts, safeguarding sensitive information, and reporting suspicious activities.

5. **Investing in Advanced Security Technologies**: Implementing advanced security technologies, such as endpoint protection, intrusion detection/prevention systems

(IDS/IPS), security information and event management (SIEM), and extended detection and response (XDR) solutions, enhances the organization's ability to detect and respond to threats.

6. **Fostering a Security-First Culture**: Directors should promote a culture where cybersecurity is a priority for all employees. This involves setting the tone at the top, encouraging open communication about security issues, and recognizing and rewarding good security practices.

Understanding cyber threats and risks is essential for board directors to fulfill their governance responsibilities effectively. By staying informed about the evolving threat landscape, conducting regular risk assessments, and implementing comprehensive risk management strategies, directors can help protect their organizations from cyber threats and ensure business continuity and resilience.

17. Building a Cybersecurity Culture

Promoting Cyber Awareness and Training

Creating a robust cybersecurity culture within an organization begins with promoting awareness and providing comprehensive training for all employees. Every individual within the organization must understand their role in maintaining cybersecurity and be equipped with the knowledge and skills to protect against cyber threats. Here are key steps to achieve this:

1. **Regular Training Programs**: Implement regular cybersecurity training programs tailored to different roles within the organization. These programs should cover fundamental concepts, current threats, and best practices. Interactive training methods, such as simulations and workshops, can enhance engagement and retention of information.

2. **Phishing Simulations**: Conduct periodic phishing simulations to test employees' ability to recognize and respond to phishing attempts. Provide immediate feedback and additional training to those who fall for simulated attacks to improve their awareness and response.

3. **Security Awareness Campaigns**: Launch ongoing security awareness campaigns that include newsletters, posters, and emails to keep cybersecurity top-of-mind. Highlight recent incidents, share tips, and celebrate employees who demonstrate exemplary security practices.

4. **Role-Specific Training**: Provide specialized training for employees in high-risk roles, such as IT staff, executives, and those with access to sensitive data. This training should

address specific threats and security measures relevant to their responsibilities.

5. **Onboarding Processes**: Integrate cybersecurity training into the onboarding process for new employees. Ensure that new hires understand the organization's security policies, procedures, and their role in maintaining security from day one.

Encouraging a Security-First Mindset

Fostering a security-first mindset involves embedding cybersecurity into the organization's culture and daily operations. This requires a top-down approach, where leadership sets the tone and all employees are encouraged to prioritize security. Here are strategies to cultivate a security-first mindset:

1. **Leadership Commitment**: Senior leaders, including board directors, must visibly support and prioritize cybersecurity. This can be demonstrated through regular communications, participation in training, and allocation of resources to security initiatives.

2. **Security Champions**: Appoint security champions within different departments to advocate for cybersecurity best practices and act as liaisons between their teams and the security function. Security champions can help reinforce training, address concerns, and promote a culture of vigilance.

3. **Incorporate Security into Business Processes**: Ensure that cybersecurity considerations are integrated into all business processes, from product development to customer service. This includes conducting security assessments during project planning and incorporating security requirements into procurement processes.

4. **Reward and Recognition Programs**: Recognize and reward employees who demonstrate exceptional commitment to cybersecurity. This can be through formal awards, public acknowledgment, or incentives. Positive reinforcement encourages others to follow suit and prioritize security.

5. **Open Communication**: Create an environment where employees feel comfortable reporting security concerns, potential threats, and incidents without fear of reprisal. Establish clear channels for reporting and ensure that reported issues are promptly addressed.

Collaboration Between IT and Other Departments

Effective cybersecurity requires collaboration between the IT department and other parts of the organization. Cybersecurity should not be seen as solely the responsibility of IT but as a collective effort involving all departments. Here are ways to promote cross-departmental collaboration:

1. **Interdepartmental Committees**: Establish interdepartmental committees or working groups focused on cybersecurity. These groups should include representatives from IT, legal, HR, finance, and other relevant departments to discuss security issues, share insights, and coordinate efforts.

2. **Clear Roles and Responsibilities**: Define clear roles and responsibilities for cybersecurity within each department. Ensure that each department understands its specific responsibilities and how they contribute to the overall security posture of the organization.

3. **Regular Communication**: Foster regular communication between the IT department and other departments through meetings, updates, and shared documentation. Encourage open dialogue about security challenges, needs, and achievements.

4. **Joint Training and Exercises**: Conduct joint training sessions and cybersecurity exercises involving multiple departments. This promotes understanding, cooperation, and readiness to respond to incidents collectively.

5. **Integrating Security into Business Objectives**: Align cybersecurity initiatives with business objectives and ensure that security considerations are part of strategic planning. This

helps all departments understand the importance of cybersecurity in achieving the organization's goals.

Building a cybersecurity culture is a critical component of effective cybersecurity governance. By promoting cyber awareness and training, encouraging a security-first mindset, and fostering collaboration between IT and other departments, board directors can create an environment where cybersecurity is embedded in the organization's DNA. This proactive approach not only enhances the organization's security posture but also contributes to its overall resilience and success.

18. Developing a Cybersecurity Strategy

Setting Cybersecurity Objectives and Goals

A well-defined cybersecurity strategy begins with establishing clear objectives and goals that align with the organization's overall mission and business objectives. These objectives should be specific, measurable, achievable, relevant, and time-bound (SMART). Here are key steps to setting cybersecurity objectives and goals:

1. **Identify Key Assets and Priorities**: Determine which assets, systems, and data are most critical to the organization's operations and success. Prioritize these elements in your cybersecurity strategy to ensure they receive adequate protection.

2. **Assess Current Security Posture**: Conduct a thorough assessment of the organization's current cybersecurity capabilities, identifying strengths, weaknesses, and gaps. This assessment should include an evaluation of existing policies, controls, and technologies.

3. **Define Risk Tolerance**: Establish the organization's risk tolerance levels, which indicate the acceptable level of risk for various assets and operations. This helps in making informed decisions about resource allocation and risk mitigation strategies.

4. **Set Specific Goals**: Develop specific cybersecurity goals based on the assessment and risk tolerance levels. Examples include reducing the number of phishing incidents by a certain percentage, improving incident response times, or achieving compliance with specific regulatory standards.

5. **Align with Business Objectives**: Ensure that cybersecurity goals align with broader business objectives and support the organization's strategic vision. This alignment helps in gaining executive support and justifying investments in cybersecurity initiatives.

Aligning Cybersecurity with Business Strategy

Integrating cybersecurity into the overall business strategy ensures that security considerations are part of decision-making processes and strategic planning. This alignment fosters a holistic approach to risk management and supports the organization's long-term success. Here are strategies to achieve alignment:

1. **Executive Involvement**: Engage senior leadership in cybersecurity planning and decision-making. Their involvement demonstrates the importance of cybersecurity and ensures that security initiatives receive the necessary support and resources.

2. **Cross-Functional Collaboration**: Foster collaboration between cybersecurity teams and other business units to integrate security considerations into all aspects of the organization's operations. This includes product development, customer service, and supply chain management.

3. **Risk-Based Approach**: Adopt a risk-based approach to cybersecurity, focusing on protecting the most critical assets and addressing the most significant threats. This approach ensures that resources are allocated efficiently and effectively.

4. **Regular Review and Adjustment**: Continuously review and adjust the cybersecurity strategy to reflect changes in the threat landscape, business priorities, and technological advancements. This ensures that the strategy remains relevant and effective.

Resource Allocation for Cybersecurity Initiatives

Adequate resource allocation is essential for implementing a robust cybersecurity strategy. This includes financial resources, personnel, and technological investments. Here are key considerations for resource allocation:

1. **Budgeting for Cybersecurity**: Ensure that the organization allocates sufficient budget for cybersecurity initiatives. This budget should cover the costs of tools, technologies, personnel, training, and compliance efforts.

2. **Investing in Technology**: Invest in advanced cybersecurity technologies that enhance the organization's ability to detect, prevent, and respond to threats. This includes firewalls, intrusion detection/prevention systems (IDS/IPS), endpoint protection, SIEM, and XDR solutions.

3. **Hiring and Training Personnel**: Recruit skilled cybersecurity professionals and provide ongoing training to keep them updated on the latest threats and best practices. This includes not only IT staff but also employees across the organization who play a role in maintaining security.

4. **Outsourcing and Partnerships**: Consider outsourcing certain cybersecurity functions to specialized providers or partnering with cybersecurity firms for additional expertise and resources. This can be particularly beneficial for small and medium-sized enterprises (SMEs) with limited in-house capabilities.

Incident Response and Disaster Recovery Planning

An effective cybersecurity strategy must include comprehensive plans for incident response and disaster recovery. These plans ensure that the organization can quickly and effectively respond to cyber incidents, minimizing damage and ensuring business continuity. Here are key components:

1. **Incident Response Plan (IRP)**: Develop an incident response plan that outlines the steps to be taken in the event

of a cybersecurity incident. This includes identifying the incident, containing the threat, eradicating the cause, recovering systems, and conducting a post-incident review.

2. **Incident Response Team (IRT)**: Establish a dedicated incident response team with clearly defined roles and responsibilities. Ensure that team members are trained and equipped to handle various types of cyber incidents.

3. **Disaster Recovery Plan (DRP)**: Develop a disaster recovery plan that focuses on restoring critical systems and operations after a significant disruption. This includes data backups, recovery procedures, and alternative work arrangements.

4. **Regular Testing and Drills**: Conduct regular testing and drills to ensure that incident response and disaster recovery plans are effective and that employees are familiar with their roles and responsibilities. This helps identify gaps and areas for improvement.

5. **Continuous Monitoring and Improvement**: Continuously monitor the effectiveness of incident response and disaster recovery efforts. Use lessons learned from past incidents to improve plans and procedures.

Developing a comprehensive cybersecurity strategy is essential for protecting the organization's assets, data, and reputation. By setting clear objectives, aligning cybersecurity with business strategy, allocating adequate resources, implementing robust policies, and planning for incident response and disaster recovery, board directors can ensure that their organization is well-prepared to face the evolving cyber threat landscape.

19. Cybersecurity Policy Making

Cybersecurity policies provide the framework for managing and protecting the organization's information assets. They establish guidelines and procedures for employees to follow, ensuring consistent and effective security practices. Here are key steps in developing and implementing cybersecurity policies:

1. **Policy Development**: Develop comprehensive cybersecurity policies that address various aspects of security, including data protection, access control, incident response, and acceptable use. Ensure that policies are clear, concise, and aligned with industry standards and regulatory requirements.

2. **Stakeholder Involvement**: Involve stakeholders from different departments in the policy development process to ensure that policies are practical, relevant, and address the needs of the entire organization.

3. **Policy Implementation**: Implement policies through training, awareness programs, and regular communications. Ensure that employees understand their responsibilities and the importance of adhering to security policies.

4. **Monitoring and Enforcement**: Establish mechanisms for monitoring compliance with cybersecurity policies and enforcing them consistently. This includes conducting regular audits, reviewing logs, and taking corrective actions when violations occur.

5. **Continuous Improvement**: Regularly review and update cybersecurity policies to reflect changes in the threat landscape, business operations, and technological advancements. This ensures that policies remain effective and relevant.

Developing Comprehensive Cybersecurity Policies

Effective cybersecurity policy making is a critical component of an organization's overall security strategy. Comprehensive policies establish clear guidelines and procedures for managing and protecting information assets, ensuring consistency and accountability across the organization. Here are key steps to develop robust cybersecurity policies:

1. **Identify Key Areas**: Determine the key areas that need to be addressed by cybersecurity policies. Common areas include data protection, access control, incident response, network security, endpoint security, and employee responsibilities.

2. **Stakeholder Involvement**: Involve stakeholders from different departments in the policy development process to ensure that policies are practical, relevant, and address the needs of the entire organization. This includes IT, legal, HR, compliance, and business unit leaders.

3. **Align with Regulations and Standards**: Ensure that cybersecurity policies comply with relevant regulations, standards, and industry best practices. This includes GDPR, HIPAA, PCI DSS, NIST, ISO/IEC 27001, and other applicable frameworks.

4. **Clear and Concise Language**: Write policies in clear and concise language that is easily understood by all employees. Avoid technical jargon and ensure that policies are accessible to non-technical staff.

5. **Define Roles and Responsibilities**: Clearly define the roles and responsibilities of employees, management, and the IT security team in maintaining and enforcing cybersecurity policies. Specify who is responsible for implementing, monitoring, and updating each policy.

6. **Review and Approval**: Draft policies should be reviewed and approved by senior management and the board of directors to ensure alignment with the organization's strategic objectives and risk tolerance.

Policy Implementation and Enforcement

Once cybersecurity policies are developed, they must be effectively implemented and enforced to ensure compliance and effectiveness. Here are key steps for successful implementation and enforcement:

1. **Communication and Training**: Communicate the policies to all employees and provide training to ensure they understand their responsibilities and the importance of adhering to security policies. Use various communication channels, such as emails, intranet, and training sessions, to reach all staff.

2. **Integration into Business Processes**: Integrate cybersecurity policies into the organization's standard operating procedures and business processes. This ensures that security considerations are part of daily operations and decision-making.

3. **Access Control and Permissions**: Implement access control measures to enforce policies related to data access and usage. This includes role-based access control (RBAC), multi-factor authentication (MFA), and regular reviews of access permissions.

4. **Monitoring and Auditing**: Establish mechanisms for monitoring compliance with cybersecurity policies. Conduct regular audits and assessments to identify non-compliance and areas for improvement. Use automated tools to track and report on policy adherence.

5. **Incident Management**: Develop procedures for managing policy violations and security incidents. This includes defining the steps to be taken in response to a breach, such as investigation, remediation, and reporting. Ensure that there are clear consequences for policy violations.

6. **Feedback and Continuous Improvement**: Create a feedback loop to gather input from employees and stakeholders on the effectiveness of policies. Use this

feedback to make continuous improvements and updates to policies as needed.

Regular Review and Updates

Cybersecurity policies must be regularly reviewed and updated to remain effective and relevant in the face of evolving threats and changes in the organization's environment. Here are key considerations for maintaining up-to-date policies:

1. **Scheduled Reviews**: Establish a regular schedule for reviewing cybersecurity policies, such as annually or biannually. This ensures that policies are consistently evaluated and updated as needed.

2. **Incident and Audit Findings**: Use findings from security incidents, audits, and assessments to inform policy updates. Analyze the root causes of incidents and identify any policy gaps or weaknesses that need to be addressed.

3. **Regulatory Changes**: Stay informed about changes in relevant regulations and standards. Update policies to ensure continued compliance with new or revised legal requirements.

4. **Technological Advancements**: Monitor advancements in technology and cybersecurity practices. Update policies to incorporate new tools, techniques, and best practices that enhance the organization's security posture.

5. **Organizational Changes**: Consider changes in the organization's structure, operations, and business objectives when updating policies. Ensure that policies remain aligned with the organization's strategic goals and risk profile.

6. **Stakeholder Input**: Involve stakeholders in the review and update process to ensure that policies remain practical and relevant. Gather input from different departments and adjust policies based on their feedback and experiences.

Examples of Cybersecurity Policies

To provide a practical framework for cybersecurity policy making, here are examples of key policies that organizations should consider developing:

1. **Data Protection Policy**: Defines how the organization protects sensitive data, including personal information, financial records, and intellectual property. Covers data classification, handling, storage, and disposal practices.

2. **Access Control Policy**: Establishes guidelines for granting, reviewing, and revoking access to systems and data. Includes requirements for authentication, authorization, and access reviews.

3. **Incident Response Policy**: Outlines the procedures for identifying, reporting, and responding to cybersecurity incidents. Defines roles and responsibilities, communication protocols, and incident handling steps.

4. **Network Security Policy**: Sets standards for securing the organization's network infrastructure. Includes guidelines for firewall configurations, intrusion detection/prevention systems, and secure network design.

5. **Endpoint Security Policy**: Defines the security measures for protecting endpoint devices, such as laptops, smartphones, and tablets. Covers antivirus software, encryption, and device management.

6. **Acceptable Use Policy**: Establishes the rules for using the organization's IT resources, including computers, internet access, and email. Defines acceptable and unacceptable behaviors and practices.

7. **Backup and Recovery Policy**: Specifies the procedures for backing up critical data and systems and the steps for restoring them in the event of a disaster. Includes backup schedules, storage locations, and recovery testing.

8. **Third-Party Risk Management Policy**: Outlines the process for assessing and managing cybersecurity risks associated with third-party vendors and partners. Includes due diligence, contract requirements, and ongoing monitoring.

Effective cybersecurity policy making is essential for establishing a secure and resilient organization. By developing comprehensive policies, ensuring effective implementation and enforcement, regularly reviewing and updating policies, and incorporating stakeholder input, board directors can create a robust framework for managing cybersecurity risks and protecting the organization's information assets.

20. Governance Structures for Cybersecurity

Roles and Responsibilities of the Board and Executive Management

Effective governance structures for cybersecurity are essential for ensuring that cybersecurity risks are managed proactively and strategically. Clear roles and responsibilities for the board of directors, executive management, and other key stakeholders are critical to establishing accountability and driving a culture of security throughout the organization.

1. **Board of Directors:**

   - **Strategic Oversight:** The board is responsible for providing strategic oversight of the organization's cybersecurity posture. This includes understanding the risks, setting the tone at the top, and ensuring that cybersecurity is integrated into the overall business strategy.

   - **Policy Approval:** The board reviews and approves major cybersecurity policies, ensuring they align with the organization's goals and regulatory requirements.

   - **Resource Allocation:** The board ensures that adequate resources—financial, technological, and human—are allocated to cybersecurity initiatives.

   - **Performance Monitoring:** The board regularly monitors cybersecurity performance through reports, key performance indicators (KPIs), and updates from the Chief Information Security Officer (CISO) or equivalent.

2. **Executive Management:**

   - **Implementation and Enforcement:** Executive management, particularly the CEO, COO, and CFO, is responsible for the implementation and enforcement of cybersecurity policies and strategies approved by the board.

   - **Operational Oversight:** Executive leaders oversee day-to-day cybersecurity operations, ensuring that the organization's cybersecurity measures are effectively protecting its assets and data.

   - **Risk Management:** Executives are responsible for identifying, assessing, and managing cybersecurity risks. They ensure that appropriate risk mitigation strategies are in place and are regularly reviewed and updated.

3. **Chief Information Security Officer (CISO):**

   - **Leadership and Strategy:** The CISO leads the cybersecurity program, developing and implementing the organization's cybersecurity strategy, policies, and procedures.

   - **Reporting:** The CISO reports regularly to the board and executive management on the state of cybersecurity, including threats, incidents, and performance metrics.

   - **Coordination and Communication:** The CISO coordinates with other departments and ensures effective communication of cybersecurity initiatives, risks, and incidents across the organization.

Establishing Cybersecurity Committees

Creating specialized committees dedicated to cybersecurity can enhance governance by providing focused oversight and expertise. These committees ensure that cybersecurity receives the attention and resources necessary to address complex and evolving threats.

1. **Cybersecurity Committee:**

   - **Purpose**: A cybersecurity committee is tasked with overseeing the organization's cybersecurity program, providing strategic direction, and ensuring alignment with business objectives.

   - **Composition:** The committee typically includes board members, senior executives, the CISO, and other relevant stakeholders. It may also include external advisors with expertise in cybersecurity.

   - **Responsibilities**: The committee reviews and approves cybersecurity policies, monitors performance, assesses risks, and ensures that appropriate mitigation strategies are in place. It also facilitates communication between the board, executive management, and the cybersecurity team.

2. **Audit and Risk Committee:**

   - **Cybersecurity Focus**: An existing audit and risk committee can incorporate cybersecurity into its mandate, focusing on the identification, assessment, and management of cybersecurity risks.

   - **Responsibilities**: The committee ensures that cybersecurity risks are included in the organization's overall risk management framework. It reviews audit reports, compliance with regulations, and the effectiveness of internal controls related to cybersecurity.

3. **Technology Committee:**

   - **Role in Cybersecurity**: A technology committee can provide oversight of the organization's technology infrastructure, including cybersecurity.

   - **Responsibilities**: The committee evaluates the organization's technological capabilities, ensures that cybersecurity considerations are integrated into technology projects, and monitors emerging technologies and their potential impact on security.

Reporting and Accountability Mechanisms

Effective reporting and accountability mechanisms are crucial for ensuring that cybersecurity efforts are transparent, measurable, and aligned with the organization's goals. These mechanisms enable the board and executive management to make informed decisions and hold stakeholders accountable for cybersecurity performance.

1. **Regular Reporting**:

   - **Frequency**: Establish regular reporting intervals for cybersecurity updates to the board and executive management. Reports can be monthly, quarterly, or as needed based on the organization's risk profile and regulatory requirements.

   - **Content**: Reports should include updates on the current threat landscape, incidents and responses, compliance status, performance metrics, and progress on strategic initiatives. Key performance indicators (KPIs) and metrics should be clearly defined and tracked over time.

2. **Dashboards and Metrics**:

   - **Real-Time Monitoring**: Implement cybersecurity dashboards that provide real-time visibility into the organization's security posture. Dashboards should display critical metrics such as incident response times, vulnerability management status, and user compliance with security policies.

   - **Key Performance Indicators (KPIs)**: Define KPIs that align with the organization's cybersecurity goals. Examples include the number of detected threats, time to detect and respond to incidents, compliance rates, and the effectiveness of training programs.

3. **Incident Reporting**:

   - **Immediate Notification**: Establish protocols for immediate notification to the board and executive management in the event of a significant cybersecurity incident. This ensures that senior leaders are aware of critical issues and can take appropriate action.

- **Post-Incident Reviews**: Conduct thorough post-incident reviews to analyze the causes, impact, and response to cybersecurity incidents. Use findings to improve policies, procedures, and controls.

4. **Compliance and Audit Reports**:

- **Internal Audits**: Conduct regular internal audits to assess compliance with cybersecurity policies and regulatory requirements. Audits should identify gaps and recommend corrective actions.

- **External Assessments**: Engage third-party auditors or assessors to provide an independent evaluation of the organization's cybersecurity posture. External assessments offer valuable insights and help ensure objectivity.

Integrating Cybersecurity into Corporate Governance

Integrating cybersecurity into the broader corporate governance framework ensures that it is treated as a critical aspect of organizational risk management and strategic planning. This holistic approach enhances the organization's resilience and ability to respond to evolving threats.

1. **Strategic Alignment:**

- **Business Objectives**: Ensure that cybersecurity strategies and initiatives align with the organization's overall business objectives. This alignment helps justify investments in cybersecurity and demonstrates its value to the organization.

- **Risk Management**: Integrate cybersecurity risk management into the organization's enterprise risk management (ERM) framework. This includes identifying cybersecurity risks as part of the overall risk assessment process and prioritizing them based on their potential impact on the organization.

2. **Board Education and Training:**

   - **Ongoing Education:** Provide ongoing education and training for board members on cybersecurity topics, including emerging threats, regulatory requirements, and best practices. This ensures that board members are well-informed and capable of making strategic decisions related to cybersecurity.

   - **Expert Briefings:** Arrange briefings from cybersecurity experts to provide the board with insights into the latest trends and developments. These briefings can include presentations from the CISO, external advisors, or industry experts.

3. **Cultural Integration:**

   - **Security-First Culture:** Promote a security-first culture throughout the organization, where cybersecurity is viewed as everyone's responsibility. Encourage employees to prioritize security in their daily activities and decision-making processes.

   - **Leadership Commitment:** Demonstrate leadership commitment to cybersecurity by integrating it into corporate values, policies, and practices. Visible support from senior leaders reinforces the importance of cybersecurity and drives cultural change.

4. **Resource Allocation:**

   - **Budgeting:** Ensure that adequate resources are allocated to cybersecurity initiatives, including funding for technology, personnel, training, and compliance efforts. Resource allocation should be based on a thorough assessment of cybersecurity needs and priorities.

   - **Human Resources:** Invest in recruiting, training, and retaining skilled cybersecurity professionals. Provide opportunities for continuous learning and professional development to keep the cybersecurity team up-to-date with the latest trends and technologies.

Establishing robust governance structures for cybersecurity is essential for managing risks and ensuring the organization's resilience in the face of evolving threats. By clearly defining roles and responsibilities, creating specialized committees, implementing effective reporting and accountability mechanisms, and integrating cybersecurity into the broader corporate governance framework, board directors can provide strategic oversight and support a culture of security throughout the organization.

21. Role of Board Directors in Cyber Risk Management

Identifying and Mitigating Cyber Risks

Board directors play a critical role in identifying and mitigating cyber risks, ensuring that the organization is protected from potential threats. Effective risk management begins with understanding the landscape of cyber threats and vulnerabilities that could impact the organization. Here are key steps directors should take in identifying and mitigating cyber risks:

1. **Understand the Threat Landscape:**

    - **Stay Informed:** Directors should stay informed about the latest cyber threats, trends, and attack vectors. This can be achieved through regular briefings from the Chief Information Security Officer (CISO), participation in cybersecurity forums, and subscription to threat intelligence services.

    - **Risk Identification:** Collaborate with the cybersecurity team to identify and categorize potential cyber risks. This includes understanding the types of threats (e.g., malware, phishing, insider threats) and the potential impact on critical assets and operations.

2. **Conduct Comprehensive Risk Assessments:**

    - **Regular Assessments:** Ensure that the organization conducts regular and comprehensive risk assessments. These assessments should evaluate the likelihood and impact of identified threats and vulnerabilities on the organization's assets, data, and operations.

- **Third-Party Assessments**: Engage external experts to conduct independent risk assessments. Third-party assessments provide an objective view of the organization's security posture and identify areas for improvement.

3. **Develop Risk Mitigation Strategies**:

- **Risk Prioritization**: Prioritize risks based on their potential impact and likelihood. Focus on mitigating high-priority risks that could significantly disrupt operations or cause substantial financial and reputational damage.

- **Implement Controls**: Develop and implement risk mitigation strategies, including technical controls (e.g., firewalls, encryption), administrative controls (e.g., policies, training), and physical controls (e.g., access restrictions, surveillance).

4. **Monitor and Review Risks**:

- **Continuous Monitoring**: Establish continuous monitoring processes to detect and respond to emerging threats and vulnerabilities. Use advanced security tools, such as Security Information and Event Management (SIEM) systems, to monitor network traffic and system logs in real-time.

- **Regular Reviews**: Conduct regular reviews of risk mitigation strategies and update them as needed. Ensure that the board receives regular updates on the organization's risk profile and the effectiveness of risk management efforts.

Risk Management Frameworks and Tools

Adopting robust risk management frameworks and tools is essential for systematically identifying, assessing, and mitigating cyber risks. These frameworks provide structured approaches and best practices for managing risks across the organization.

1. **NIST Cybersecurity Framework**:

NIST Cybersecurity Framework provides a comprehensive approach to managing cybersecurity risk through five core functions- **Identify,**

Protect, Detect, Respond, Recover: The. Directors should ensure that the organization's risk management practices align with this framework.

2. **ISO/IEC 27001**:

ISO/IEC 27001 is an international standard for establishing, implementing, maintaining, and continually improving **Information Security Management System (ISMS)**. Directors should support the adoption of ISO/IEC 27001 to ensure a systematic approach to managing information security risks.

3. **COBIT (Control Objectives for Information and Related Technologies)**:

COBIT provides a framework for **IT governance and management**, emphasizing risk management, control objectives, and performance measurement. Directors should promote the integration of COBIT principles into the organization's risk management practices.

4. **Enterprise Risk Management (ERM)**:

ERM frameworks, such as COSO ERM, provide a holistic and integrated approach to managing risks across the organization. Directors should ensure that cybersecurity risks are integrated into the broader ERM framework, allowing for a comprehensive view of organizational risks.

Integrating Cyber Risk into Enterprise Risk Management

Integrating cyber risk into the organization's Enterprise Risk Management (ERM) framework ensures that cybersecurity is treated as a critical component of overall risk management. This approach promotes a unified and strategic view of risks across the organization.

1. **Unified Risk Management:**

   - **Holistic View**: Treat cybersecurity as an integral part of the overall risk landscape. Directors should ensure that cyber risks are evaluated alongside other business risks, such as financial, operational, and strategic risks.

- **Cross-Functional Collaboration:** Encourage collaboration between the cybersecurity team and other departments, such as finance, operations, and legal, to identify and manage interrelated risks.

2. **Risk Appetite and Tolerance:**

- **Define Risk Appetite:** Work with executive management to define the organization's risk appetite and tolerance levels for cybersecurity. This helps in making informed decisions about resource allocation and risk mitigation strategies.

- **Align with Business Objectives:** Ensure that the organization's cyber risk management practices align with its strategic goals and business objectives. This alignment helps in prioritizing risks and making decisions that support long-term success.

3. **Risk Reporting and Metrics:**

- **Key Risk Indicators (KRIs):** Establish key risk indicators to monitor and report on the organization's cyber risk exposure. KRIs provide early warning signs of potential risks and help in proactive risk management.

- **Regular Reporting:** Implement regular reporting mechanisms to keep the board and executive management informed about the organization's cyber risk profile. Reports should include updates on risk assessments, mitigation efforts, and emerging threats.

Incident Response and Crisis Management

Effective incident response and crisis management are essential components of cyber risk management. Board directors must ensure that the organization is prepared to respond swiftly and effectively to cyber incidents, minimizing damage and ensuring business continuity.

1. **Incident Response Planning:**

   - **Develop Response Plans:** Ensure that the organization has a comprehensive incident response plan (IRP) in place. The IRP should outline roles, responsibilities, and procedures for detecting, responding to, and recovering from cyber incidents.

   - **Regular Testing:** Conduct regular testing and simulations of the incident response plan to ensure that it is effective and that all stakeholders are familiar with their roles and responsibilities.

2. **Crisis Management Team:**

   - **Establish a Team:** Form a dedicated crisis management team comprising key stakeholders, including the CISO, IT staff, legal, communications, and executive management. The team should be prepared to coordinate the organization's response to major cyber incidents.

   - **Clear Communication:** Develop clear communication protocols for internal and external stakeholders during a crisis. Ensure that timely and accurate information is provided to employees, customers, partners, regulators, and the media.

3. **Post-Incident Review:**

   - **Conduct Reviews:** After each significant incident, conduct a thorough post-incident review to analyze the response, identify areas for improvement, and update the incident response plan accordingly.

   - **Learn from Incidents:** Use lessons learned from incidents to enhance the organization's risk management practices and strengthen its cybersecurity posture.

Board directors have a vital role in managing cyber risks and ensuring the organization's resilience in the face of evolving threats. By identifying and mitigating risks, adopting robust risk management frameworks, integrating cyber risk into the ERM framework, and ensuring effective incident response and crisis management, directors can provide strategic oversight and support a proactive approach to cybersecurity risk management. This comprehensive approach helps protect the organization's assets, reputation, and long-term success.

22. Incident Response and Disaster Recovery

Effective incident response and disaster recovery planning are essential components of a robust cybersecurity strategy. These plans ensure that an organization can swiftly and effectively respond to cybersecurity incidents, minimize damage, and restore normal operations. Board directors play a crucial role in overseeing and supporting these efforts to ensure organizational resilience and continuity.

Developing and Implementing Incident Response Plans

An incident response plan (IRP) outlines the steps an organization must take to detect, respond to, and recover from cybersecurity incidents. A well-structured IRP helps minimize the impact of incidents and ensures a coordinated and efficient response.

1. **Establish an Incident Response Team (IRT):**

    - **Team Composition:** Form an IRT comprising members from various departments, including IT, legal, HR, communications, and executive management. The team should include individuals with the expertise and authority to make critical decisions during an incident.

    - **Roles and Responsibilities:** Clearly define the roles and responsibilities of each team member. Ensure that everyone understands their duties and the chain of command during an incident.

2. **Define Incident Types and Severity Levels:**

    - **Classification:** Categorize potential incidents based on their nature (e.g., malware, phishing, DDoS) and severity (e.g., low, medium, high). This helps prioritize response efforts and allocate resources appropriately.

- **Impact Assessment**: Establish criteria for assessing the impact of an incident on the organization's operations, data, and reputation. This assessment guides decision-making and response actions.

3. **Incident Detection and Reporting**:

- **Detection Mechanisms**: Implement tools and technologies to detect cybersecurity incidents, such as intrusion detection systems (IDS), security information and event management (SIEM) solutions, and network monitoring.

- **Reporting Procedures**: Develop clear procedures for reporting incidents, including internal reporting channels and timelines. Ensure that employees know how and when to report suspicious activities.

4. **Response Procedures**:

- **Containment**: Outline steps to contain the incident and prevent further damage. This may include isolating affected systems, blocking malicious traffic, and disabling compromised accounts.

- **Eradication**: Define procedures for eradicating the threat, such as removing malware, closing vulnerabilities, and eliminating unauthorized access.

- **Recovery**: Detail the steps for restoring affected systems and data to normal operations. This includes verifying the integrity of restored systems and ensuring that they are free from compromise.

5. **Communication Plan**:

- **Internal Communication**: Establish protocols for communicating with internal stakeholders, including employees, management, and the board. Provide timely updates on the incident status and response efforts.

- **External Communication:** Develop a plan for communicating with external stakeholders, such as customers, partners, regulators, and the media. Ensure that messaging is consistent, transparent, and compliant with legal and regulatory requirements.

6. **Training and Drills:**

- **Regular Training:** Conduct regular training sessions for the IRT and other relevant personnel to ensure they are familiar with the IRP and their roles during an incident.

- **Simulation Exercises:** Perform regular simulation exercises and tabletop drills to test the effectiveness of the IRP and identify areas for improvement. These exercises should cover various incident scenarios and involve all relevant stakeholders.

Crisis Management, Business Continuity and Disaster Recovery

Crisis management and business continuity planning are integral to an organization's resilience. These plans ensure that the organization can continue critical operations and recover quickly after a significant disruption.

1. **Crisis Management Framework:**

- **Crisis Management Team:** Establish a dedicated crisis management team responsible for coordinating the organization's response to major incidents. This team should include senior leaders and representatives from key departments.

- **Crisis Communication Plan:** Develop a crisis communication plan that outlines how the organization will communicate with internal and external stakeholders during a crisis. Ensure that the plan includes pre-approved messaging templates and contact lists.

2. **Business Impact Analysis (BIA):**

   - **Identify Critical Functions:** Conduct a BIA to identify critical business functions and processes that must be maintained or quickly restored during a disruption.

   - **Assess Impact:** Evaluate the potential impact of various types of disruptions on these critical functions, including financial, operational, and reputational impacts.

3. **Business Continuity Plan (BCP):**

   - **Develop BCP:** Create a comprehensive BCP that outlines the strategies and procedures for maintaining and restoring critical business functions. The BCP should address various scenarios, including cyber incidents, natural disasters, and other emergencies.

   - **Resource Allocation:** Identify the resources required to implement the BCP, including personnel, technology, and facilities. Ensure that these resources are readily available and can be mobilized quickly.

4. **Disaster Recovery Plan (DRP):**

   - **Develop DRP:** Develop a disaster recovery plan that focuses on restoring IT systems, data, and infrastructure following a major disruption. The DRP should include detailed procedures for backup, recovery, and system validation.

   - **Regular Testing:** Conduct regular testing of the DRP to ensure its effectiveness. This includes testing backup and recovery processes, validating recovery time objectives (RTOs), and ensuring that recovery procedures are up-to-date.

5. **Continuous Improvement:**

   - **Post-Incident Reviews:** After each incident, conduct a post-incident review to analyze the response, identify lessons learned, and improve the IRP, BCP, and DRP. Use these insights to enhance the organization's resilience and preparedness.

- **Regular Updates:** Regularly review and update the IRP, BCP, and DRP to reflect changes in the organization's operations, technology, and threat landscape. Ensure that these plans remain relevant and effective.

Key Metrics and Reporting

Effective incident response and disaster recovery require continuous monitoring and reporting to track progress, measure effectiveness, and ensure accountability.

1. **Key Performance Indicators (KPIs):**

- **Incident Detection and Response Time:** Measure the time taken to detect and respond to incidents. Track metrics such as mean time to detect (MTTD) and mean time to respond (MTTR) to assess the efficiency of response efforts.

- **Impact Assessment:** Monitor the impact of incidents on the organization's operations, data, and reputation. Track metrics such as the number of affected systems, data loss, and financial costs.

2. **Reporting Mechanisms:**

- **Regular Reports:** Provide regular reports to the board and executive management on the status of incident response and disaster recovery efforts. These reports should include updates on incidents, response activities, and recovery progress.

- **Post-Incident Analysis:** Conduct detailed post-incident analysis and reporting to identify strengths and weaknesses in the response and recovery processes. Use these insights to drive continuous improvement.

3. **Compliance and Audit:**

   - **Regulatory Compliance:** Ensure that incident response and disaster recovery efforts comply with relevant regulations and standards. Track compliance metrics and address any gaps or deficiencies.

   - **Internal and External Audits:** Conduct regular internal and external audits of the IRP, BCP, and DRP to ensure their effectiveness and identify areas for improvement.

Disaster Recovery Planning and Execution

In today's digital age, businesses rely heavily on information technology to operate effectively and efficiently. However, this dependence comes with significant risks, including cyber threats, natural disasters, and human errors. Therefore, having a robust disaster recovery plan (DRP) in place is essential for any organization to ensure business continuity and minimize downtime in the face of unforeseen disruptions.

The Importance of Disaster Recovery Planning

Disaster recovery planning is a strategic approach to preparing for, mitigating, and recovering from disruptions. In the context of cybersecurity, it involves developing protocols and procedures to protect data, maintain essential services, and quickly restore normal operations following a cyber incident or other types of disruptions.

Benefits of Disaster Recovery Planning:

1. **Minimized Downtime:** A well-structured DRP ensures that essential systems and services are restored quickly, reducing the duration of downtime.

2. **Data Protection:** Implementing regular backups and data redundancy strategies helps safeguard critical information against loss or corruption.

3. **Business Continuity:** Ensures that business operations can continue or resume rapidly, maintaining customer trust and preventing revenue loss.

4. **Regulatory Compliance:** Many industries are subject to regulations that require specific disaster recovery measures. A DRP ensures compliance with these legal requirements.

5. **Risk Mitigation:** Identifies potential risks and outlines preventive measures, reducing the likelihood of disasters and their impact on business operations.

Key Components of a Disaster Recovery Plan

An effective disaster recovery plan should encompass several key components, each tailored to the organization's unique needs and vulnerabilities:

1. **Risk Assessment and Business Impact Analysis (BIA):**

- **Risk Assessment:** Identify and evaluate potential threats, such as cyberattacks, natural disasters, hardware failures, and human errors.

- **Business Impact Analysis (BIA):** Determine the impact of different disaster scenarios on critical business functions and prioritize recovery efforts based on their importance.

2. **Recovery Objectives:**

- **Recovery Time Objective (RTO):** The maximum acceptable length of time that a system or service can be offline.

- **Recovery Point Objective (RPO):** The maximum acceptable amount of data loss measured in time. This determines how frequently data backups should occur.

3. **Data Backup and Restoration:**

   - **Regular Backups:** Implement frequent backups of critical data and systems to secure offsite or cloud-based storage.

   - **Data Integrity Checks:** Regularly verify the integrity and reliability of backups to ensure they are not corrupted or compromised.

4. **Disaster Recovery Sites:**

   - **Primary and Secondary Sites:** Establish alternate locations where critical operations can be shifted in case of a primary site failure.

   - **Cloud Solutions:** Utilize cloud-based disaster recovery services for scalable and cost-effective solutions.

5. **Communication Plan:**

   - **Internal Communication:** Develop clear communication channels and protocols for notifying employees about the disaster and recovery steps.

   - **External Communication:** Prepare templates and strategies for communicating with customers, partners, and stakeholders during and after a disaster.

6. **Incident Response Team:**

   - **Team Composition:** Assemble a dedicated team responsible for executing the DRP, including IT professionals, security experts, and key business leaders.

   - **Roles and Responsibilities:** Clearly define the roles and responsibilities of each team member to ensure coordinated and efficient recovery efforts.

7. **Testing and Maintenance:**

- **Regular Testing:** Conduct regular drills and simulations to test the effectiveness of the DRP and identify areas for improvement.

- **Plan Updates:** Continuously review and update the DRP to address new threats, technological changes, and organizational growth.

Execution of a Disaster Recovery Plan

The execution phase of a disaster recovery plan involves activating the protocols and procedures outlined in the plan. This phase can be broken down into several critical steps:

1. **Incident Detection and Assessment:**

- **Early Detection:** Use monitoring tools and systems to detect incidents promptly.

- **Impact Assessment:** Quickly assess the severity and impact of the incident to determine the appropriate response.

2. **Plan Activation:**

- **Decision Making:** The incident response team decides to activate the DRP based on the assessment.

- **Notification:** Communicate the activation to all relevant parties, including employees, customers, and stakeholders.

3. **Data Recovery and System Restoration:**

- **Backup Retrieval:** Retrieve and restore data from backups based on the RTO and RPO objectives.

- **System Restoration:** Rebuild and restore affected systems and services to operational status.

4. **Communication and Coordination:**

   - **Internal Coordination:** Ensure effective communication and coordination among the incident response team and other internal departments.

   - **External Updates:** Provide regular updates to customers, partners, and stakeholders about the recovery progress.

5. **Post-Recovery Review:**

Incident Analysis: Conduct a thorough analysis of the incident to identify root causes and areas for improvement.

Plan Revision: Update the DRP based on lessons learned to enhance future preparedness and resilience.

Disaster recovery planning and execution in cybersecurity are paramount for safeguarding business continuity and protecting critical assets. By developing a comprehensive DRP that includes risk assessment, data backup strategies, communication plans, and regular testing, organizations can effectively mitigate the impact of disasters and ensure rapid recovery. In an era where cyber threats and other disruptions are increasingly prevalent, a robust disaster recovery plan is not just a necessity but a strategic advantage.

As the threat landscape continues to evolve, organizations must remain vigilant and proactive in their approach to incident response and disaster recovery. Emerging trends and technologies, such as artificial intelligence, machine learning, and automation, offer new opportunities to enhance these efforts. By staying informed and continuously improving their strategies, organizations can build a robust and resilient cybersecurity posture that protects their assets, data, and reputation. Board directors must prioritize incident response and disaster recovery as key components of the organization's overall cybersecurity strategy. By developing comprehensive plans, fostering a culture of preparedness, and leveraging advanced technologies, directors can ensure that their organization is well-equipped to handle any disruption and emerge stronger and more resilient.

23. Cybersecurity Metrics and Reporting

Key Performance Indicators (KPIs) for Cybersecurity

Effective measurement and reporting of cybersecurity performance are essential for ensuring accountability, driving continuous improvement, and providing visibility into the organization's security posture. Key Performance Indicators (KPIs) are metrics used to evaluate the effectiveness of cybersecurity efforts and to identify areas needing attention. Here are some critical KPIs that board directors should consider:

1. **Incident Detection and Response:**

   - **Mean Time to Detect (MTTD):** The average time it takes to identify a cybersecurity incident. Shorter MTTD indicates more effective detection capabilities.

   - **Mean Time to Respond (MTTR):** The average time it takes to respond to and mitigate an incident after detection. A lower MTTR signifies efficient incident response processes.

   - **Incident Volume:** The total number of detected incidents over a specific period. Monitoring trends in incident volume helps identify emerging threats and the effectiveness of preventive measures.

2. **Vulnerability Management:**

   - **Patch Management Effectiveness:** The percentage of systems with up-to-date patches and the average time to apply patches after release. This KPI reflects the organization's ability to manage vulnerabilities proactively.

- **Vulnerability Closure Rate**: The rate at which identified vulnerabilities are remediated. A high closure rate indicates effective vulnerability management.

3. **User Awareness and Training**:

- **Phishing Simulation Success Rate**: The percentage of employees who successfully identify and report phishing simulations. This metric measures the effectiveness of security awareness training.

- **Training Completion Rate**: The percentage of employees who have completed mandatory cybersecurity training. High completion rates suggest strong organizational commitment to cybersecurity education.

4. **Access Control and Authentication**:

- **Multi-Factor Authentication (MFA) Adoption**: The percentage of systems and accounts protected by MFA. Higher adoption rates enhance security by reducing the risk of unauthorized access.

- **Failed Login Attempts**: The number of failed login attempts, which can indicate potential brute force attacks or credential misuse.

5. **Data Protection and Privacy**:

- **Data Loss Incidents**: The number of incidents involving data loss or unauthorized data access. Monitoring this KPI helps assess the effectiveness of data protection measures.

- **Encryption Coverage**: The percentage of sensitive data that is encrypted, both in transit and at rest. Higher coverage rates indicate better data protection practices.

Reporting Cybersecurity Metrics to the Board

Regular reporting of cybersecurity metrics to the board is essential for maintaining transparency, enabling informed decision-making, and demonstrating the effectiveness of cybersecurity initiatives. Here are best practices for reporting cybersecurity metrics to the board:

1. **Establish Reporting Frequency:**

   - **Regular Updates:** Provide regular cybersecurity updates to the board, typically on a quarterly basis. More frequent reporting may be necessary during periods of heightened threat or following significant incidents.

   - **Ad Hoc Reporting:** Deliver ad hoc reports as needed for critical incidents or emerging threats that require immediate board attention.

2. **Use Clear and Concise Communication:**

   - **Executive Summaries:** Start with an executive summary that highlights key findings, trends, and action items. This ensures that board members can quickly grasp the most important information.

   - **Visual Aids:** Use visual aids, such as charts, graphs, and dashboards, to present metrics clearly and concisely. Visual representations help board members understand complex data more easily.

3. **Focus on Strategic Metrics:**

   - **Relevance to Business Goals:** Focus on metrics that are directly relevant to the organization's strategic goals and risk management priorities. Avoid overwhelming the board with too many technical details.

   - **Trend Analysis:** Highlight trends over time to show progress, emerging risks, and areas requiring improvement. Trend analysis provides context and helps the board understand the broader implications of the metrics.

4. **Provide Context and Actionable Insights**:

- **Contextual Information**: Provide context for the reported metrics, such as industry benchmarks, recent incidents, and changes in the threat landscape. This helps the board understand the significance of the metrics.

- **Recommendations**: Offer actionable recommendations based on the reported metrics. Highlight areas needing attention, proposed actions, and expected outcomes to guide the board's decision-making.

Using Metrics for Decision-Making and Oversight

Cybersecurity metrics play a vital role in enabling the board to make informed decisions and exercise effective oversight. Here's how metrics can be used in the decision-making process:

1. **Risk Management and Resource Allocation**:

- **Prioritizing Risks**: Use metrics to identify and prioritize cybersecurity risks. Focus resources on the highest-risk areas and ensure that mitigation efforts are aligned with the organization's risk tolerance.

- **Budget Decisions**: Metrics provide evidence to support budget requests for cybersecurity initiatives. Demonstrating the effectiveness of current investments and highlighting areas needing additional resources helps justify funding decisions.

2. **Performance Evaluation**:

- **Assessing Effectiveness**: Evaluate the effectiveness of cybersecurity initiatives by comparing current metrics to established benchmarks and goals. Use this assessment to identify successful strategies and areas needing improvement.

- **Continuous Improvement**: Foster a culture of continuous improvement by using metrics to track progress and drive enhancements in cybersecurity practices. Regularly review and update metrics to reflect changes in the threat landscape and organizational priorities.

3. **Regulatory Compliance and Reporting:**

- **Compliance Tracking:** Ensure that the organization meets regulatory requirements by tracking compliance-related metrics. Report compliance status to the board and address any gaps or deficiencies promptly.

- **Regulatory Reporting:** Use metrics to fulfill regulatory reporting obligations. Provide accurate and timely information to regulators, demonstrating the organization's commitment to cybersecurity and compliance.

4. **Incident Response and Recovery:**

- **Incident Analysis:** Use metrics to analyze the response to cybersecurity incidents. Assess the effectiveness of incident detection, containment, eradication, and recovery efforts to identify lessons learned and improve future responses.

- **Post-Incident Reviews:** Conduct post-incident reviews using metrics to evaluate the impact of incidents and the success of recovery efforts. Use insights from these reviews to update incident response plans and enhance overall resilience.

Effective measurement and reporting of cybersecurity metrics are essential for maintaining a robust security posture and enabling informed decision-making by the board. By establishing relevant KPIs, providing regular and clear reports, and using metrics to guide strategic decisions and oversight, board directors can ensure that their organization is well-equipped to manage cyber risks and protect its critical assets. This proactive approach to cybersecurity governance fosters a culture of accountability, transparency, and continuous improvement.

24. Engaging with External Experts

Engaging with external experts is a vital component of a comprehensive cybersecurity strategy. External experts provide specialized knowledge, objective assessments, and valuable insights that can enhance an organization's security posture. Board directors must ensure that their organization leverages these resources effectively to address complex cybersecurity challenges.

Collaborating with Cybersecurity Consultants and Advisors

Cybersecurity consultants and advisors offer specialized expertise and experience that can help organizations improve their cybersecurity defenses, address specific challenges, and stay ahead of emerging threats.

1. **Assessing Needs and Selecting Experts:**

   - **Identify Requirements**: Determine the specific areas where external expertise is needed, such as risk assessment, incident response, compliance, or advanced threat detection.

   - **Vet Potential Experts**: Select consultants and advisors with proven track records, relevant certifications, and experience in your industry. Consider recommendations, case studies, and client testimonials.

2. **Engagement Models:**

   - **Project-Based Engagements**: Hire consultants for specific projects, such as conducting a risk assessment, developing a cybersecurity strategy, or implementing new security technologies.

- **Ongoing Advisory Services**: Engage advisors on a retainer basis to provide continuous support, strategic guidance, and regular assessments. This model ensures ongoing access to expert advice.

3. **Maximizing Value from Consultants**:

- **Clear Objectives**: Define clear objectives, deliverables, and timelines for each engagement. Ensure that consultants understand the organization's goals and expectations.

- **Collaboration with Internal Teams**: Foster close collaboration between external experts and internal teams. Encourage knowledge transfer and capacity building to enhance internal capabilities.

- **Monitoring and Evaluation**: Regularly review the progress and outcomes of consulting engagements. Assess the impact of their recommendations and ensure that they align with the organization's strategic priorities.

Leveraging Industry Partnerships and Networks

Industry partnerships and networks offer opportunities for collaboration, information sharing, and mutual support in addressing cybersecurity threats. Engaging with these networks enhances the organization's ability to respond to threats and stay informed about the latest trends and best practices.

1. **Joining Industry Groups and Associations**:

- **Professional Associations**: Participate in professional associations such as the Information Systems Security Association (ISSA), ISACA, and the Cybersecurity and Infrastructure Security Agency (CISA). These associations provide access to resources, training, and networking opportunities.

- **Sector-Specific Groups**: Join sector-specific groups that focus on the unique cybersecurity challenges faced by your industry. For example, financial institutions can join the

Financial Services Information Sharing and Analysis Center (FS-ISAC).

2. **Information Sharing and Threat Intelligence**:

- **Threat Intelligence Platforms**: Subscribe to threat intelligence platforms that provide real-time information on emerging threats, vulnerabilities, and attack methods. Use this intelligence to enhance your organization's defenses.

- **Information Sharing Communities**: Engage in information sharing communities where members share insights, experiences, and best practices. Collaborate on threat analysis, incident response, and mitigation strategies.

3. **Collaborative Initiatives**:

- **Joint Exercises and Drills**: Participate in joint cybersecurity exercises and drills with industry partners. These activities help test and improve incident response capabilities and foster collaboration.

- **Research and Development**: Collaborate with academic institutions, research organizations, and other companies on cybersecurity research and development projects. This can lead to innovative solutions and advancements in security technologies.

Understanding the Role of External Audits and Assessments

External audits and assessments provide an objective evaluation of an organization's cybersecurity posture. They help identify gaps, validate compliance, and ensure that security measures are effective and aligned with industry standards.

1. **Types of Audits and Assessments**:

- **Compliance Audits**: Conduct audits to ensure compliance with relevant regulations and standards, such as GDPR, HIPAA, PCI DSS, and ISO/IEC 27001. Compliance audits verify that the organization meets legal and regulatory requirements.

- **Security Assessments**: Perform comprehensive security assessments, including vulnerability assessments, penetration testing, and security architecture reviews. These assessments identify weaknesses and provide recommendations for improvement.

2. **Selecting Auditors and Assessors**:

- **Qualifications and Experience**: Choose auditors and assessors with the necessary qualifications, certifications (e.g., CISSP, CISA, CEH), and experience in your industry. Ensure they have a thorough understanding of the regulatory landscape and best practices.

- **Independence and Objectivity**: Ensure that auditors and assessors are independent and objective. Avoid conflicts of interest by selecting external experts who are not involved in the implementation of the organization's security measures.

3. **Preparing for Audits and Assessments**:

- **Documentation and Evidence**: Prepare comprehensive documentation and evidence of your cybersecurity policies, procedures, and controls. Ensure that all relevant information is readily available for review.

- **Internal Reviews**: Conduct internal reviews and mock audits to identify and address potential issues before the external audit. This helps ensure a smooth audit process and better outcomes.

4. **Post-Audit Actions**:

- **Address Findings and Recommendations**: Review the findings and recommendations from the audit or assessment. Develop and implement action plans to address identified gaps and improve security measures.

- **Continuous Improvement**: Use the insights gained from audits and assessments to drive continuous improvement in your cybersecurity program. Regularly review and update policies, procedures, and controls based on audit results.

Engaging with Legal and Regulatory Experts

Legal and regulatory experts provide critical guidance on compliance with cybersecurity laws and regulations. Their expertise ensures that the organization meets legal requirements and mitigates legal risks associated with cybersecurity incidents.

1. **Understanding Regulatory Requirements**:

- **Legal Frameworks**: Stay informed about relevant legal frameworks and regulations that impact your organization, such as GDPR, CCPA, HIPAA, and industry-specific regulations.

- **Compliance Strategies**: Develop compliance strategies and policies to meet legal requirements. Legal experts can provide advice on interpreting regulations and implementing appropriate measures.

2. **Incident Response and Legal Considerations**:

- **Data Breach Notification**: Ensure that your incident response plan includes legal considerations for data breach notification. Legal experts can guide you on when and how to notify affected parties, regulators, and other stakeholders.

- **Litigation and Liability**: Understand the potential legal implications of cybersecurity incidents, including litigation and liability risks. Legal experts can help assess these risks and develop strategies to mitigate them.

3. **Contracts and Vendor Management**:

- **Third-Party Agreements**: Review contracts with third-party vendors and service providers to ensure they include appropriate cybersecurity provisions. Legal experts can help draft and negotiate terms that protect the organization's interests.

- **Data Protection Agreements**: Ensure that data protection agreements with partners and vendors comply with relevant regulations. Legal experts can assist in drafting and reviewing these agreements.

Engaging with external experts is a strategic imperative for organizations seeking to enhance their cybersecurity posture and stay ahead of evolving threats. By collaborating with cybersecurity consultants, leveraging industry partnerships, conducting external audits, and seeking legal and regulatory guidance, board directors can ensure that their organization benefits from specialized knowledge and objective insights.

This proactive approach not only strengthens the organization's defenses but also fosters a culture of continuous improvement and resilience. Board directors play a crucial role in overseeing these engagements, ensuring that the organization remains vigilant, compliant, and prepared to address the complex challenges of cybersecurity. Through effective engagement with external experts, organizations can achieve a robust and adaptive cybersecurity strategy that supports long-term success and sustainability.

25. Examples of Practical Scenarios

Understanding practical scenarios involving cybersecurity incidents helps illustrate the real-world application of cybersecurity principles and the importance of a robust cybersecurity strategy. These scenarios highlight different aspects of cybersecurity, demonstrating how organizations can effectively respond to and manage incidents.

Examining real-world case studies of cybersecurity incidents provides valuable insights and practical lessons that organizations can apply to enhance their own cybersecurity strategies. These case studies highlight both successful responses and areas for improvement, offering a comprehensive view of how different organizations manage cyber threats.

Here are four practical scenarios:

Scenario 1: A Cybersecurity Disaster Averted

Background: A large financial institution detected unusual network activity that suggested an imminent cyberattack. The institution had recently updated its cybersecurity policies and implemented advanced threat detection systems.

Response:

1. **Early Detection**: The institution's Security Operations Center (SOC) identified the unusual activity through their newly implemented SIEM system which flagged multiple unauthorized login attempts from different locations.

2. **Immediate Containment**: The incident response team quickly isolated the affected systems to prevent the spread of the potential threat.

3. **Investigation and Analysis**: A thorough investigation revealed that a sophisticated phishing campaign was underway, targeting employees to gain access to critical systems.

4. **Preventive Measures**: The institution rolled out an urgent awareness campaign, reinforcing training on phishing detection and implementing additional email filtering mechanisms.

Outcome:

- The proactive measures and swift response prevented the cyberattack from occurring, protecting sensitive financial data and maintaining customer trust.

- The institution's investment in updated cybersecurity policies and advanced detection systems proved invaluable.

Lessons Learned:

- **Proactive Measures**: Regular updates to cybersecurity policies and investment in advanced technologies can significantly enhance an organization's ability to detect and prevent attacks.

- **Employee Training**: Continuous awareness and training programs are critical in equipping employees to recognize and respond to phishing attempts effectively.

Scenario 2: Effective Incident Management and Damage Mitigation

Background: A healthcare provider experienced a ransomware attack that encrypted critical patient data. The attack threatened to disrupt operations and compromise patient care.

Response:

1. **Incident Response Activation:** The organization immediately activated its incident response plan, involving the crisis management team and external cybersecurity experts.

2. **Data Restoration:** The IT team worked to restore data from secure backups, minimizing downtime and ensuring continuity of patient care.

3. **Communication:** Clear and transparent communication was maintained with patients, regulators, and the media, explaining the situation and steps being taken to resolve it.

4. **Legal and Regulatory Compliance:** Legal experts were consulted to ensure compliance with data breach notification laws and to handle potential legal implications.

Outcome:

- The organization successfully restored operations within 48 hours, with minimal impact on patient care.

- Transparent communication helped maintain trust with patients and stakeholders.

Lessons Learned:

- **Backup and Recovery:** Regular backups and a tested disaster recovery plan are crucial for minimizing downtime and data loss during a ransomware attack.

- **Crisis Communication:** Effective communication strategies can help manage stakeholder expectations and maintain trust during a cyber incident.

Scenario 3: Enhancing Cyber Resilience Through Board Initiatives

Background: A manufacturing company faced increasing cyber threats but had weak cybersecurity measures in place. The board recognized the need for a comprehensive cybersecurity overhaul.

Response:

1. **Board-Led Initiative**: The board established a cybersecurity committee to oversee the development and implementation of a robust cybersecurity strategy.

2. **Investment in Technology**: Significant investments were made in advanced cybersecurity technologies, including endpoint protection, network security, and continuous monitoring systems.

3. **Policy Development**: Comprehensive cybersecurity policies were developed, covering data protection, access control, incident response, and employee training.

4. **Employee Engagement**: A company-wide cybersecurity awareness program was launched to educate employees about best practices and their role in maintaining security.

Outcome:

- The company saw a significant reduction in cyber incidents and an overall improvement in its security posture.

- The board's proactive approach fostered a culture of security throughout the organization.

Lessons Learned:

- **Board Involvement**: Active involvement and leadership from the board are essential in driving comprehensive and effective cybersecurity initiatives.

- **Culture of Security**: Engaging employees and fostering a culture of security are critical components of a successful cybersecurity strategy.

Scenario 4: Cybersecurity Breach and Legal Ramifications

Background: An e-commerce company suffered a major data breach that exposed customer payment information, leading to potential legal and regulatory consequences.

Response:

1. **Incident Response Activation**: The company activated its incident response plan, involving internal teams and external legal and cybersecurity experts.

2. **Customer Notification**: Affected customers were promptly notified, and measures were taken to assist them in mitigating potential fraud.

3. **Regulatory Reporting**: The company reported the breach to relevant regulatory bodies in compliance with legal requirements.

4. **Post-Incident Review**: A thorough post-incident review was conducted to identify the root cause and prevent future breaches.

Outcome:

- The company faced regulatory fines and lawsuits but managed to mitigate the damage through swift and transparent actions.

- The post-incident review led to significant improvements in security practices and policies.

Lessons Learned:

- **Regulatory Compliance**: Understanding and complying with regulatory requirements is crucial in managing the aftermath of a data breach.

- **Post-Incident Improvements**: Conducting a thorough post-incident review and implementing necessary improvements can help prevent future incidents and strengthen security.

These case studies illustrate the importance of proactive measures, effective incident response, board involvement, and regulatory compliance in managing cybersecurity threats. By learning from these real-world examples, organizations can enhance their own cybersecurity strategies and better prepare for potential incidents.

Board directors play a critical role in ensuring that the organization adopts best practices, invests in necessary technologies, and fosters a culture of security. Through continuous learning and improvement, organizations can build resilience against cyber threats and protect their assets, data, and reputation.

26. Future Trends in Cybersecurity

As the digital landscape continues to evolve, so too do the threats and challenges that organizations face. Keeping abreast of future trends in cybersecurity is crucial for board directors to ensure that their organizations remain resilient and capable of defending against emerging threats. Here are some key trends shaping the future of cybersecurity:

Emerging Technologies and Their Impact on Cybersecurity

The rapid advancement of technology brings both opportunities and challenges for cybersecurity. Organizations must understand the implications of these emerging technologies to harness their benefits while mitigating associated risks.

1. **Artificial Intelligence (AI) and Machine Learning (ML):**

   - **Enhanced Threat Detection:** AI and ML can analyze vast amounts of data to identify patterns and anomalies indicative of cyber threats. These technologies improve the speed and accuracy of threat detection and response.

   - **Automated Defense Mechanisms:** AI-powered tools can automate responses to common cyber threats, reducing the burden on human analysts and enhancing the efficiency of incident response.

2. **Internet of Things (IoT):**

   - **Increased Attack Surface:** The proliferation of IoT devices expands the attack surface, introducing new vulnerabilities. Securing IoT ecosystems requires robust device management, encryption, and network segmentation.

- **Data Privacy Concerns**: IoT devices often collect and transmit sensitive data, raising privacy concerns. Organizations must implement stringent data protection measures and ensure compliance with privacy regulations.

3. **5G Networks**:

- **Faster Data Transmission**: The rollout of 5G networks enables faster data transmission and connectivity. However, the increased speed and bandwidth also present new challenges for securing communications and data.

- **New Threat Vectors**: 5G technology introduces new threat vectors, such as network slicing and edge computing, requiring innovative security solutions to address these risks.

4. **Blockchain Technology**:

- **Data Integrity and Transparency**: Blockchain technology enhances data integrity and transparency through its decentralized and immutable ledger. It can be used to secure transactions, supply chains, and identity management.

- **Smart Contracts**: The use of smart contracts on blockchain platforms introduces security challenges, such as vulnerabilities in the code. Organizations must ensure rigorous testing and auditing of smart contracts.

Preparing for Future Cyber Threats

Anticipating and preparing for future cyber threats is essential for maintaining a robust security posture. Organizations must adopt proactive strategies to stay ahead of evolving threats and adapt to the changing threat landscape.

1. **Advanced Persistent Threats (APTs)**:

- **Sophisticated Attacks**: APTs are highly sophisticated, targeted attacks often carried out by nation-states or organized crime groups. These attacks aim to gain prolonged access to networks and steal sensitive information.

- **Threat Hunting**: Implementing proactive threat hunting practices can help detect and mitigate APTs. This involves continuously searching for indicators of compromise (IoCs) and unusual activity within the network.

2. **Ransomware Evolution:**

- **Targeted Ransomware:** Ransomware attacks are becoming more targeted, focusing on high-value organizations and demanding larger ransoms. Attackers often use advanced techniques to evade detection and maximize impact.

- **Ransomware Defense Strategies**: Organizations should implement comprehensive defense strategies, including regular backups, network segmentation, employee training, and incident response planning.

- **Supply Chain Attacks:** Cybercriminals exploit vulnerabilities in third-party suppliers to infiltrate networks and compromise data. These attacks can propagate through interconnected networks, affecting multiple organizations. Implementing robust supply chain risk management practices, such as vetting vendors, monitoring third-party access, and ensuring secure integration points, is crucial to mitigate these risks.

- **Business Operations Attacks:** Cyberattacks targeting critical business operations, such as manufacturing processes or logistics systems, aim to disrupt operations and cause financial losses. Developing resilience plans that include business continuity measures, disaster recovery protocols, and comprehensive incident response strategies can minimize the impact of such attacks and ensure swift recovery.

By focusing on these additional aspects of cyber threat preparation alongside existing strategies, organizations can enhance their resilience against a diverse range of future cyber threats.

AI-Powered Cybersecurity Platforms:

As cyber threats grow more sophisticated, traditional security measures often fall short of providing the robust defense required. This is where AI-powered cybersecurity platforms come into play, offering an advanced, adaptive, and proactive approach to safeguarding digital assets.

Understanding AI in Cybersecurity

AI powered platforms are revolutionizing the cybersecurity and digital defense. Artificial Intelligence (AI) in cybersecurity leverages machine learning (ML), deep learning, natural language processing (NLP), and other AI technologies to enhance threat detection, response, and prevention. These systems analyze vast amounts of data, identify patterns, and predict potential security incidents with unprecedented accuracy and speed.

Key Features of AI-Powered Cybersecurity Platforms

1. Advanced Threat Detection

AI systems can analyze and learn from historical data to recognize patterns indicative of cyber threats. This enables them to detect anomalies and potential threats in real-time, often before they can cause harm.

2. Automated Response and Mitigation

AI-driven platforms can automate responses to identified threats, reducing the time between detection and action. This rapid response capability is crucial in minimizing damage during a cyber-attack.

3. Predictive Analytics

Predictive analytics use historical data to forecast future threats. AI can identify vulnerabilities within systems and suggest preventive measures, helping organizations stay one step ahead of cybercriminals.

4. **Behavioral Analysis**

AI can monitor user behavior and establish baselines for normal activity. Any deviation from this baseline can trigger alerts, helping to identify insider threats and compromised accounts.

5. **Integration with Existing Systems**

Modern AI cybersecurity platforms can seamlessly integrate with existing IT infrastructure, enhancing overall security without the need for extensive overhauls.

Prominent AI-Powered Cybersecurity Platforms

1. **Sequretek's Percept XDR + NG SIEM**

Sequretek's platform combines Extended Detection and Response (XDR) with Next-Generation Security Information and Event Management (NG SIEM) to offer comprehensive network detection and response (NDR) capabilities. It excels in identifying and mitigating complex threats across various network segments.

2. **Zscaler**

Zscaler leverages AI to provide secure internet access and private application access for users, regardless of their location. Its AI-driven threat intelligence continuously updates to defend against the latest threats.

3. **Okta**

Okta utilizes AI for identity management and access control, ensuring that only authorized users can access sensitive information. Its AI algorithms analyze login patterns and behaviors to detect and prevent unauthorized access.

4. **CrowdStrike**

CrowdStrike's AI-powered Falcon platform provides endpoint protection through advanced threat detection and incident response.

Its AI algorithms analyze data from millions of endpoints to identify threats and provide actionable insights.

5. SecureWorks

SecureWorks' AI-driven platform offers comprehensive threat detection and response services. It uses machine learning to analyze threat data and automate responses, helping organizations stay ahead of potential attacks.

6. Rubrik

Rubrik's AI-powered data security platform focuses on data management and protection. It uses AI to detect ransomware attacks, ensuring that data can be quickly restored without paying ransoms.

Benefits of AI-Powered Cybersecurity

Efficiency and Accuracy
AI systems can process vast amounts of data quickly and accurately, reducing the likelihood of false positives and negatives.

Proactive Defense
Predictive analytics and real-time threat detection allow organizations to adopt a proactive stance, addressing vulnerabilities before they can be exploited.

Scalability
AI platforms can scale with the growing needs of an organization, ensuring consistent protection as digital footprints expand.

Cost-Effective
By automating routine security tasks and improving detection accuracy, AI reduces the need for large security teams, leading to cost savings.

AI-powered cybersecurity platforms represent the cutting edge of digital defense, offering enhanced protection through advanced threat detection, automated response, and predictive analytics. As cyber threats become more sophisticated, the adoption of AI in cybersecurity will be crucial for organizations seeking to safeguard their digital assets effectively. By integrating AI technologies, businesses can ensure a robust, adaptive, and proactive security posture, ready to meet the challenges of the digital age.

The Role of Board Directors in Shaping the Future of Cybersecurity

Board directors play a pivotal role in shaping the organization's cybersecurity strategy and ensuring preparedness for future threats. Their leadership and oversight are crucial for fostering a culture of security and driving continuous improvement.

1. **Strategic Oversight:**

   - **Vision and Direction**: Directors must provide strategic vision and direction for the organization's cybersecurity initiatives. This includes aligning cybersecurity goals with overall business objectives and ensuring that cybersecurity is a priority at the executive level.

   - **Resource Allocation**: Ensuring adequate resources—financial, technological, and human—are allocated to cybersecurity efforts is critical. Directors should advocate for investments in advanced technologies and skilled personnel.

2. **Continuous Learning and Adaptation:**

   - **Staying Informed**: Directors must stay informed about emerging cyber threats and technological advancements. This involves attending industry conferences, engaging with cybersecurity experts, and participating in continuous education programs.

   - **Adaptive Strategies**: Cybersecurity strategies must be adaptive and responsive to changing threats. Directors should encourage regular reviews and updates of cybersecurity policies, procedures, and technologies.

3. **Fostering a Culture of Security:**

   - **Leadership Commitment:** Directors should demonstrate a strong commitment to cybersecurity, setting the tone at the top and ensuring that cybersecurity is integrated into the organization's culture.

   - **Employee Engagement:** Engaging employees at all levels in cybersecurity initiatives is essential. This includes regular training, awareness programs, and encouraging a proactive approach to identifying and reporting security issues.

4. **Collaboration and Information Sharing:**

   - **Industry Collaboration:** Directors should promote collaboration with industry peers, government agencies, and cybersecurity organizations. Sharing information and best practices can enhance the collective defense against cyber threats.

   - **Public-Private Partnerships:** Engaging in public-private partnerships can provide access to valuable resources, threat intelligence, and support from government and industry bodies.

The future of cybersecurity is shaped by rapidly evolving technologies, sophisticated threats, and the need for proactive and adaptive strategies. Board directors have a crucial role in guiding their organizations through this complex landscape, ensuring that they are prepared to face emerging challenges and capitalize on new opportunities.

By staying informed, fostering a culture of security, and promoting continuous improvement, directors can help their organizations build a resilient cybersecurity posture. Embracing innovation and collaboration will be key to navigating the future of cybersecurity and safeguarding the organization's assets, data, and reputation. Through strategic leadership and a commitment to excellence, board directors can drive their organizations toward a secure and successful future.

27. Epilogue

As we conclude, it is clear that the digital revolution has ushered in an era of unparalleled opportunities and unprecedented challenges. The integration of AI and AI powered intelligent automation systems, with robust cybersecurity platforms represents the future of safeguarding our digital enterprises. This synergy not only enhances the protective measures but also ensures a proactive stance against the ever-evolving threat landscape.

The regulatory environment, with laws like Sarbanes-Oxley (SOX) and the SEC's new requirement for breach disclosure within four business days, underscores the critical importance of transparency and accountability. These regulations serve as both a guiding light and a stern reminder for organizations to prioritize cybersecurity at the highest levels of governance. The repercussions and penalties for non-compliance highlight the need for a comprehensive and dynamic approach to cybersecurity, one that is deeply embedded in the corporate fabric.

Throughout this journey, we have examined the strategic, operational, and technological dimensions of cybersecurity. From understanding the foundational principles to learning about advanced cybersecurity technologies, the narrative has been anchored on the premise that cybersecurity is not a destination but an ongoing process. It demands vigilance, innovation, and a relentless commitment to staying ahead of cyber adversaries.

The role of intelligent automation in this domain cannot be overstated. AI-powered solutions are transforming the way we detect, respond to, and mitigate cyber threats. By automating routine tasks, identifying patterns, and predicting potential breaches, these systems enable human experts to focus on strategic decision-making and complex problem-solving. This collaboration between human intelligence and machine learning epitomizes the future of cybersecurity.

However, as we look ahead, it is crucial to recognize that technology alone cannot secure our digital future. A holistic approach that encompasses people, processes, and technology is essential. Training and awareness programs, robust governance frameworks, and a culture of security must complement technological advancements. Only then can we build resilient organizations capable of withstanding the sophisticated cyber threats of tomorrow.

A crucial component of this holistic approach is the role of the board of directors in strengthening cybersecurity. Board members must understand the gravity of cyber risks and actively engage in shaping the organization's cybersecurity strategy. Their oversight ensures that adequate resources are allocated, appropriate policies are enacted, and a culture of security is fostered throughout the organization. By championing cybersecurity at the highest level, boards can drive meaningful change and bolster the company's resilience against cyber threats.

In conclusion, the journey of cybersecurity is one of continuous learning and adaptation. As we forge ahead in this digital age, let us embrace the transformative power of intelligent automation and advanced cybersecurity platforms. Let us commit to fostering a culture of security and resilience, where every stakeholder understands their role in protecting our digital assets. By doing so, we not only safeguard our enterprises but also contribute to a safer, more secure digital world for all.

The future of cybersecurity is bright, but it requires our collective efforts to navigate the complexities and seize the opportunities that lie ahead. Let us move forward with confidence, vigilance, and a shared commitment to excellence in cybersecurity. Thank you for joining me on this journey.

www.ingramcontent.com/pod-product-compliance
Lightning Source LLC
Chambersburg PA
CBHW072017230526
45479CB00008B/73